BUDDHISM

BUDDHISM

A STORY OF THE BUDDHIST NORM

By

MRS. RHYS DAVIDS, M.A.

Lecturer in Indian Philosophy, Manchester University

Fellow of University College, London

GYAN

Published by

Gyan Publishing House
5, Ansari Road
Daryaganj, New Delhi-110002
Phone: 011-47034999, 9811692060
E-mail: books@gyanbooks.com

Distribution Network
gyanbooks.com
India, USA, Canada, UK, Australia, France

ISBN: 978-81-212-3171-8 (PB)
First Published,

2nd Impression 2020

Printed at: Gyan Press, Delhi.

Buddhism: A Story of the Buddhist Norm
Author: Mrs. Rhys Davids

CONTENTS

BUDDHISM

CHAPTER I

THE PALI TRADITION

THE general growth of interest in Buddhism is due to more than one assignable cause. But we may class the various causes fairly enough under the growth of general knowledge. And under this fact of expanding knowledge we may distinguish between growth of intellectual curiosity and sympathy in the knower, and additional facilities in the means of knowing.

We must resist the temptation, in the limited scope at our disposal, of lingering over the former group of causes, and glance forthwith at the latter.

In the first place we are now beginning to reap the harvest sown by certain pioneers, who returned last century from countries where creed and culture are or have been Buddhist, in their hearts the wish, on their shoulders the task, to make known in the West a literature venerable in its tradition, and, where still followed, a living force in the present, but practically unknown outside

Asia. This was the religious literature of Ceylon, Siam, and Burma, written on palm-leaf manuscripts, and, for the most part, in a language not at any time native to any of those countries, but hailing from the ancient dialects of North-East India. Closely akin to this language, which, as a literary diction, is known in the mediæval portion of the literature as *pāli* (or The Text), is that of certain inscriptions carved on rock and pillar, found in different parts of India. These are known as the Edicts of the Emperor Asoka, the Indian over-lord who reigned *about* 272-35 B.C. They consist largely of injunctions to righteous and fraternal conduct, and refer to passages contained in the most ancient of these same Pāli compositions. These oldest compilations are treasured, in the three countries above-named, as canonical scriptures. And the Pāli language is judged to be a literary version of an Indo-European or Aryan dialect, later than the language of the Vedas and Brāhma*n*as, or oldest known Brahmin texts, but earlier than what is called Sanskrit, that is, the literary language of India during nearly the whole of the Christian era.

Now this Pāli was the vehicle of what is, so far as we have yet been able to discover, the earliest formulated records of Buddhism. Dead as a vernacular, it still lives on as a literary instrument in the native colleges or monasteries of Ceylon, Siam, and Burma, just as Latin was the mediæval, and is, to some extent still, the modern vehicle for ecclesiastical Christianity. In its vernacular or spoken form, it appears to have been the language, according to Buddhist commentarial tradition, of Măg'ădhă, according to Rhys Davids, of Kôsălă, about the fifth century B.C. (or earlier) and subsequent centuries. It was in the kingdom of Kosala that the Buddhist movement took firmest root, growing up in the great college at Sāvatthī, the site of which has during the last few years been excavated. So that although the first Buddhist Emperor, Asoka, was of Magadha, south of Kosala, and established his capital at Patna on the Ganges, the Buddhist canon had already been compiled (though not yet written) more or less in its present form in Kosalese, and not in Māgadhī, and so it has since then remained in the countries of Further India, after the expulsion of Buddhism from its birthplace.

Buddhism was a missionizing movement from the first, and Further India was won over to Buddhism by missions dispatched from its centres in North-East India. And it is in Further India, constantly loyal to its adopted religion, that the Pāli books, handwritten on palm-leaves, have been preserved, freshly copied, commented upon, or otherwise elaborated in other palm-leaf manuscripts, and have thence, in copies old or new, been sold or given to, or appropriated by Europeans.

Now while Prinsep on the one hand first deciphered the rock-cut inscriptions of the Emperor Asoka, containing historical evidence of inestimable value, Turnour, Childers and Gogerly, Oldenberg and Rhys Davids, for over half a century, have been educating European culture in the contents of the Pāli palm-leaf MSS. Prior to this, our knowledge of early Buddhism was derived from certain books of an early mediæval date, such as that from which the late Edwin Arnold derived his famous poem, " The Light of Asia." These books were written in the Sanskrit, which as a *general literary* vehicle of thought (and not as merely the language of a learned class) had gradually superseded the earlier literary vehicle of Pāli. So far, no manuscripts from Northern India, or from Buddhist centres North and North-East of India, have yielded us anything, in diction or in subject-matter, so apparently near to the beginnings of Buddhism, as a religion and a body of culture, as some of these Pāli books that Ceylon, Siam and Burma have preserved. These oldest books, together with several of a somewhat later date, claim, by their own testimony, and the ancient tradition of these southern Buddhist countries, to have been collected into a Canon or Bible of sacred documents, entitled the *Three Pit'ăkăs*, or *Baskets of Tradition*. They were, and are, held " sacred " in this sense, that they are believed to contain the genuine sayings of Go'tămă, the Buddha, the founder of Buddhism, as well as other books, which are elaborations of subjects stated by him in outline; sacred also in this, that they may not be added to, nor otherwise altered.

Besides these Three Pitakas, the Pāli literature contains a great body of exegetical commentary on the Pitakas, mainly as to the oldest group of it, the work of two scholars, both Indian—Buddhaghosa and Dhammapāla—dating from the fifth century, A.D. a great number of sub-commentaries added gradually from that date till the present, and lastly a number of other treatises, some older and some more recent than the great commentaries. These are independent works, in that they are not systematic expositions of the sacred texts. But they are, again, dependent in that they express opinions in conformity with those texts, and frequently cite them as authoritative.

Now it is the editing of this palm-leaf literature in printed books, and the translating of them by the scholars I have named, aided by many others, that has been gradually, for the last half century, bringing a knowledge of early Buddhism to the educated public in Europe and America. The Pāli Text Society alone, founded by Professor Rhys Davids in 1881, has published seventy volumes of texts and translations. *The Sacred Books of the East*, founded by the late Max Müller, published several translations. *The Sacred*

Books of the Buddhists series, the Harvard *Oriental Series*, the German *Pali-Society* are publishing more.

Recent political events in Asia have also aided in bringing Buddhism nearer to us. The annexation of Upper Burma by Great Britain in 1889 resulted in bringing a number of Government officials and European teachers to reside in, and become acquainted with, Burma and its religion and culture. French and English interference in Siam has had a somewhat similar result. And the rise of Japan, as a great power among the Great Powers, has set Europe considering the part played in that rise by the Buddhist factor in Japanese religion. Lastly, the secrets of the cult of Tibet—a curious adulterated Buddhism—and of its ecclesiastical libraries, seem at length to be becoming a little less inaccessible to us. More than this one cannot say, but the additional factor in the general interest in Buddhism remains.

Once more, there is the awakening to new and international activity in Buddhist countries, in connection with their own religion and culture, that must be taken into account. More than two thousand years after the period of its first missionary zeal, we hear, simultaneously from all the five countries named above, of fresh movements, not only of self-defence against the invasion of other creeds, but also of attack.

Of these movements the system of ultramontane, chiefly political propaganda, started by the Tibetan Church is well known to exist and may have important results at least in Asia, but at present of those results, or of its organization we can say nothing, and its effective influence for Europe is as yet *nil*. Elsewhere the new activity is purely religious, and consists chiefly in (1) the printing of the canonical and other Pāli classical works in the national script; (2) the inclusion of these and other printed books in the monastic manuscript libraries; (3) the increase of Buddhist colleges; (4) the establishment of foreign missions; (5) the circulation of periodical propagandist literature in East and West; (6) the institution of societies, chiefly in the West, for the study of Buddhism.

Whatever may be the final result of the opening up of so many avenues, political, geographical, literary and educational, the immediate consequences involve a wider acquaintance among ourselves with Buddhists and with all the varieties of their traditions and culture as Buddhists.

But that wider acquaintance will profit us little, in so far as we honestly wish to get a just idea of those traditions and an intelligent appreciation of that culture, if we rigidly estimate the one or the other by the measure of our own traditional standpoints. These standpoints have been slowly built up in the past by a certain selection among notions and beliefs. Some we threw away; some we adopted; and from time to time we made alterations or reforms. And where we altered, we found it not always possible to make our traditions of speech conform to our reforms. For instance, we have ceased to believe that the sun "rises" or "sets." We *believe* that when each of those events happens, our portion of earth rolls sunwards, and away from the sun, respectively, in its rotation around its own axis and the sun. But the old phrases hold firm, so that we should expect to hear even our astronomers use them.

These facts, then:—a specific tradition in knowledge, and a vehicle of expression that has not coincided in its growth with the growth of that knowledge—should make us wary in estimating another tradition, another standpoint, other modes of expression. We may fancy that we are measuring other views by standpoints that are not only absolutely true, but the only standpoints possible or conceivable. But in fact we are measuring, by what is relatively true, by what has come to be accepted among ourselves as true, a different range of standpoints, which have come to hold good, analogously and equally, for other sections of humanity.

And it is just the otherness in standpoint, in the midst of much that is like our own, that we need to discern before we judge, and from which, in contributing unit-wise to modify the thought of our day, we have most to learn.

It is not the purpose of this little book to repeat the story of the origin and growth of Buddhism, as revealed in the life and teaching of him whom Buddhists and their books adore as its founder. This has been repeatedly told, in every language of Europe, and the telling of it adapted to all classes of readers. Most of us have read, in some form, the story of the wonderful noble of North-East India, known as Go'tămă, the Buddha, or Siddhattha, or Sākyamuni,[1] and of the Church or community of religious brethren, and of lay-followers founded by him, and by him taught and guided for the last forty years of his entirely devoted life. A scholar here and there has sought to explain away the legend of the Buddha's renunciation and ministry as an evolution and adaptation of that great group of fantasies entitled sun-myths. But since these explanations were attempted, the pile of historic evidence, archæological and documentary, has been ever growing, till at this time of day we may say that the life of Siddhattha Gotama of the Sākyas, as a historical fact, is at least as well demonstrated as that of the founder of any other religion of any antiquity.

Draped and embroidered with myth and legend it is, no less than the story of every

[1] Siddhattha (Sanskrit, Siddhartha) Gotama = personal and family names; Sākyamuni, sage or saint of the Sākyans, his clan; Buddha = Awakened, Enlightened, Wise, a title equivalent to our Messiah or Christ.

such founder's life. But a personal mission extending over years, devolving on to, and carried on by unbroken apostolic succession, till as an organized institution it was accepted for centuries as the paramount religious guide in the culture of India, is a stubborn thing to argue away. The acceptance of it as, in the main, historically true may show a less extravagant recourse to forced interpretations, and assumptions of improbable happenings, than the denial of it as such.

Be that as it may, about the existence of a tradition of culture, religious, philosophical, ethical, handed down by that apostolic succession till this day in Southern Asia with remarkable purity and consistency, there can be no reasonable question whatever. Here too, it is true, a few sceptical minds have suggested that the documents attesting this unbroken tradition of events alleged to have happened in North-East India were not originally compiled *soon after*, and *there*, as they claim to have been, but were composed much later, in the earliest home of their creed's adoption, to wit, in Ceylon. They are therefore only the pious romancing of religious writers in the Buddhist monasteries of that island, working on a basis of stored-up runes and legends.

It is true that the Pāli Canon was not committed to writing till long after it had existed as an unwritten compilation, and till nearly two hundred years after Buddhism had been introduced into Ceylon. This last-named event took place in the year 241 B.C.; the writing down of the Canon began about 80 B.C. But it is well known that, in India, memory and oral tradition have ever been considered a safer method of protecting sacred doctrines from the introduction and perpetuation of errors than writing. We read, in the Pāli Canon itself, of how the Brahmins in India met, in certain towns at stated intervals, to con over their own unwritten hymns and prayers. And even the hearing of these was jealously guarded from certain castes. Even at the present day, it is we, and not the Hindus, who need the written letter of their sacred literature. And it was an innovation when the Buddhists of Ceylon, fearing lest the brutal hand of war, in a small island, might at any moment crush out the existence of these splendidly trained memories, decided to make use of the secular art of writing, wherewith to register their mental stores. And so we read in the two classic chronicles of Ceylon :—

> The brethren wise of former days, they handed down by word of mouth
> The Text of the Three Pit'akas, and all the Commentary too.
> Seeing how men were perishing, the brethren then together came,
> And that the Faith might be maintained, made writing of the Law in Books.

There is no evidence in any portion of this literature either in Pitaka or Commentary, that this late recourse to writing was due to any mystery-mongering or esotericism. The Buddha, it is stated, said that his was not the hand of a teacher, closed now and again to withhold doctrines. The teaching was adapted to the listener: milk for babes, strong meat for those who were strong. But this was all.

No one then who knew anything of these "memory-libraries," as a remarkable feature of past and present Indian culture, would judge the Pāli books to be late, and quasi-spurious documents because, as *written records*, they came into being more than four centuries after their adherents claim that they were compiled. It is the fact that there is no surviving tradition of the Buddhist Churches in India taking similar steps, when their existence was threatened, that has helped to throw doubt on the authenticity of the Pāli books as genuine North-East Indian compilations, put together some in the fourth, some in the third century, before Christ.

The whole question of the history of Pāli-classic literature is far from being settled. But that it is a question of deep interest for philology, for the history of writing, for the history of Indian culture, for the history of religion, is coming at last to be recognized. And it is they who most deeply study the literature who tend to be convinced that, in the Canon or Three Pitakas, we have no *literary* production composed far away, in space and time, from the centre of the movement of which it tells, but an accretion of works, compiled as the geologist would say, *in situ*, and at different dates, and at different centres, with variations, not in doctrines, but in degree of emphasis on this and that doctrine. The absence of symmetry and of system in its structure, its imperfectly coinciding repetitions, its variety of diction, all testify against its being wholly the work of a remote, late, provincial centre. The folk-lore with which it abounds is of that great stock which made its way out of North-West India into Europe. The similes with which it abounds are those of a sub-tropical continent and a great river-valley, rather than those of a tropical island. The scenes and places are North-East Indian, and may fairly be said to be described or alluded to as things seen.

The history of Pāli literature does not exhaust the question of Buddhist literature. But so far as we know, it does cover the history of the original Canon of Buddhist doctrine, considered as Canon. By Canon I mean any document or group of documents handed down, by persons acknowledged to be authoritative teachers, as containing the doctrine they teach, and, as to its contents, considered *closed*. In India itself have survived a few early works by Buddhists, written in a transitional diction between the earlier Pāli or Kosalan, and the encroaching later Sanskrit; and a few works in purer Sanskrit,

But the great majority of Buddhist works, other than those that the Southern centres have preserved as Canonical, and have themselves added, are to be found in China, translated into Chinese. It is from re-translations of these into English, French or German—and this is the great task before the newer generation of Buddhist scholars—that we may expect to enrich our knowledge of classic Buddhist literature. From the Tibetan libraries too, when these become more accessible, we may yet win materials. But we may not hope to discover there, or in China, a Buddhist literary tradition handed down in unbroken continuity from the third century B.C., like that of the Pāli Canon in Ceylon.

From the following century China began to incline to the teaching of Buddhism, and from then till the seventh century we read of scholars and pilgrims going or returning to China laden with Buddhist literature. But meanwhile from the parent trunk, represented by the teaching of the Pāli Canon, there was growing out the great limb of divergent doctrines and sects known as Mahā-Yānist Buddhism. This—the "Great Vehicle"—first rivalled, then outgrew the mother Church, which became known among the daughters as Hīna-Yāna: Little (or Low) Vehicle. And it is these departures in Buddhism that appealed most effectively to the mission Churches in China, Korea, and Japan, and which became further differentiated—how we do not yet know—into the cult, so far removed from the canonical teaching, of the Lamaism of Tibet.

It can hardly be reasonably doubted, in the absence of any historical testimony, that this great and growing division in Indian Buddhism as a religious institution must have greatly aided the hostile advance of Brahminism during the early centuries of the Christian era. Buddhism started from its birth as a religious movement among the laity, as distinct from that class called Brahmins, who possessed privileges from of old, to wit, a monopoly of erudition in sacred runes, hymns, doctrine, and spells, and of the right to celebrate priestly rites. Its first converts were drawn largely from the noble or warrior class (*khaṭṭiya*'s, Sanskrit: *kshatriya*'s). But the majority among this class were unfit to appreciate the intellectual and ethical standpoints of the new doctrine. "Whence," the Buddha is said to ask a novice who had tried his 'prentice hand at teaching a young noble, "whence should Jāyasena, born and bred in the pursuit of worldly and sensuous desires, know and see and realize that which can only be known and seen and realized by coming out of it all? 'Tis like two friends walking hand in hand into the country till, coming to a crag, one climbs up, the other stays below and calls: 'What see you up there?' And he hears: 'I see up here a lovely garden, a lovely wood, a lovely landscape, a lovely lake.' He answers:

'That's impossible.' But the other drags him up. . . ."[1]

No creed needed so much as Buddhism to be left severely alone by political patronage, and to work out its slowly permeating and leavening effect undisturbed by ignorance in high places. But just as, in the Protestant Reformation, with the assumption by civil rulers of states of the headship over the reformed Churches, there went along with it a great advance of organization, discipline, and propaganda in the Roman Church; so in India, under Asoka, the development of the khattiyas into the new imperialism of civil and (virtually) religious headship over India, was met by a corresponding consolidation of Brahmin tradition and influence. Gods and heavens and beliefs as to the soul and its destiny had undergone no little modification, since first their Aryan ancestors brought the Vedic hymns into India. Nevertheless the religious ritual upheld by the Brahmins met a chronic popular demand relatively ignored by Buddhism. It gave ceremonial dignity and sacramental sanction to all the vital features of physical and social life. Hardly may any religion endure as solely sufficient, that does not recognize and enhance the ordinary life of man in all its aspects.

If in the long run its political allies proved bad friends, Indian Buddhism, in the philosophical aberration of its degeneracy, went far

[1] *Majjhima-Nikāya*, iii, 129 *f.*

to surrender itself into the hands of its foes. It abandoned its own original trend of philosophy, and went off to a side-track which has figured so greatly in such metaphysic as this country has produced—the question of the reality of the external world. And thus, as Dr. Walleser has recently pointed out,[1] by over-emphasizing the negation of that reality, it played up to what we should now call the Absolutist position of its Vedântist opponents, namely, that the only reality behind the illusions which our senses bring us, is the soul in man and in the universe. Dr. Walleser holds that the consequent victory of Brahminism over Buddhism was thus won by intellect and logic. And he is right by the extent to which the Buddhist schools in India were unfaithful to their earlier philosophical position.

To this we may return later. We need not here dwell on the story, told elsewhere, in manuals on Buddhism, of the decline and expulsion of that which once, as cult and culturew, as paramount in India, gathering under its wing the learning and the science, the philosophy and the literature, the ethics and the social melioration of its age. The evidence as to episodes of persecution at the hands of certain rājas and Brahmins in the days when Buddhism was going under, is so far not firmly based. Equally scanty as yet is our knowledge of the decline and fall of

[1] *Der ältere Vedânta*, Heidelberg, 1910.

the Asokan empire, of the extension of Buddhism to Kashmir under the patronage of the Scythian king, Kanishka, or of its shrinkage elsewhere in India back to its earlier centres in and around Magadha, the nucleus of Asoka's dominion. Were it not for the invaluable records left by the three famous Chinese Buddhist pilgrims who visited the chief seats of Buddhist, that is, Indian culture —Fa-Hien in A.D. 400, Sung Yun in A.D. 518, and Yuan-Chwang in A.D. 629-648—the darkness would be yet greater than it is. When the Buddhist and Jain literature of this period—*i.e.*, of the centuries just before, and the first four after the beginning, of our era—shall have emerged from their chrysalis-state of manuscript; when archæological research shall be carried on in a way befitting our rule in India, we may at length be able to construct something like a continuous history

If I have alluded, even in the barest outline, to the historical fact of the waning of Buddhist paramountcy in India, it was in order the better to limit and simplify the scope of our inquiries in the following pages. The reader should never forget that to treat of "Buddhism" is just as complex and many-sided as to treat of "Christism," or, as we have selected to say, of "Christianity." The latter subject admits of very different treatment according to the aspect selected, the period of time, the centre of development, and so on. To the best of my belief, no European writer has ever been called upon to deal, even in outline, with the whole subject of Christianity or Christendom in a book of this compass. It is equally impracticable to do so in the case of Buddhism, By the foregoing the reader will see that, under that title, a book might be written with equal pertinence either on the story of the inception of the Buddhist movements and its legends, on the Buddhism of the Pāli Canon, on the history of that Canon, on the Mahā-Yānist evolution, on schools of Buddhist philosophy, on Buddhist India, on Trans-Indian Buddhism, and so forth.

It is true that these subjects are not mutually independent. As with Christianity so here, but one Founder is acknowledged, and but one and the same cradle land. And that which we have seen called the Lower Vehicle, but which should, with greater historical propriety, be called by its more ancient name of the Theravāda, or School of the Elders or Apostles, is by all admitted to be the parent stem. No Mahā-Yānist, however, and no Lamaist would concede that any treatment entitled "Buddhism" was adequate, that did not show the history of the doctrine as a progressive inspiration, and their own cult as the expanded and perfect flower of the parent gospel.

And more: the range of the subject of Buddhism is not to be confined to the cult and its adherents. India could not for a time have so far adopted that cult that we may speak of Buddhist India, and of Buddhist thought and culture, as temporarily Indian thought and culture, without being indelibly modified by it. The influence of Buddhist religion and philosophy on the post-Buddhistic Indian literature is well marked. In the words of St. Paul (1 Cor. xiii., 11) when the Indian was a child, he understood as a child, he reasoned as a child. But when, under the influence of Buddhism, he became for a while a man, he put away youthful things, at least to this extent, that the graver and more virile concepts of Theravāda Buddhism may be heard reverberating through the later devotional and philosophical literature of India, even of schools opposed to Buddhism. Very forcibly was it said by the late Edmund Hardy: "Buddhism wasted away after rival sects had appropriated everything from it that they could make any use of." (*Indische Religionsgeschichte*, 101.)

It will now be seen that some selection in this vast subject is necessary, if the slender bulk of this volume is to contain anything less superficial than a general outline of the whole. And in selecting, for this reason, and in choosing, as I have done, to present some considerations on the philosophical concepts contained in the Pāli Canon and subsequently developed, it is chiefly for these reasons :—Based on that Canon, a philosophical tradition has been, in the Buddhist countries of Southern Asia, evolved and has survived, as a living vehicle of culture, to the present day. Even then, if we find no complete and finished "system" of philosophy in those old books of the Theravāda, we should find what is of greater interest than any such system. We should find either the more tentative output of *original* fetches of the mind, or, at least, the adopted concepts of still older strata of thought. It is not the pioneers of intellectual expansion who give us systems, but they whose fate it was to be, as the Greeks said, After-born (*epigonoi*). But in either case, in the history of human ideas, it cannot be anything but deeply interesting to consider those ideas which have served as the roots of a living philosophical tradition over 2,000 years old. Our own is of about the same age, for did we not inherit it and assimilate it from Greek sources? In and through that tradition we have learnt to regard life and the world and our fellow-creatures and the human mind. But are there other fundamental standpoints from which we *might have come* to regard them?

We are apt to think there are not. We judge that, because the bed-rock of man's animal life is the same in every one:—life, death, sex, the passions—he will not vary in his fundamental beliefs and judgments. But these, in so far as they are *reasoned*, represent the accumulated heritage, bequeathed to the whole world, *or* a section of it, by its most gifted minds—the minds of the creators of points of view, and of their "after-born"—and accepted. Now it may happen that one section of humanity may *not* have accepted some such fresh point of view. Some other new synthesis may have extruded it, or the section was not ripe for it. The new view of things may have been, in the judgment of another section of humanity, or of the same section, elsewhere in time, sounder, truer, than its then successful rivals. But the "conjuncture," as the Germans say, passed by. The point of view, if it had been accepted, or if it had been put forward elsewhere among mankind, might have modified the whole trend of any one tradition of thought to an indefinite degree.

What actually has happened is that, in the first place, the general view of things underlying this and that group of human beliefs has not developed along one and the same line. The differences may be not so much in the notions conceived, as in the emphasis or proportion of weight attached to them. This difference becomes a very telling factor in the religious or philosophical superstructure. Secondly, these underlying notions themselves are not the same everywhere and at all times.

Now that the Pāli Pitakas—let alone the tradition *directly* inherited from them—can claim to show any originality in philosophical departure, that they can, on any ground, claim to occupy a place in the general history of philosophy, save at best as a degenerate offshoot of earlier syntheses—this is not yet allowed. "The more we advance in Central

Asiatic research," wrote the late Professor R. Pischel, " the clearer it appears that, for a great portion of the Orient, Buddhism was not less a vehicle of culture than Christianity has been for the Occident. While Buddhism, he goes on to say, " as a religion gains (by that research) ever in value, as a philosophy it sinks ever deeper. With Garbe and Jacobi I am convinced that Buddha as a philosopher is entirely dependent on Kapila and Patañjali." That is to say, such philosophical concepts as we may meet with in the Buddhist doctrines of the Pāli Canon—for Pischel admits that these are the oldest, if only " the canon of one Buddhist sect," and uses them as his authorities—are derived from works attributed to two philosophers so named. The works in question are the Sānkhya Aphorisms and the Yogasūtra—also a collection of aphorisms. Of the two thinkers, Kapila and Patañjali, as historical characters, there is no sound surviving evidence, and the works in question appear enshrined in commentaries, the earliest of which are a good deal subsequent to the Christian era. But tradition ascribes to the original utterances considerably greater antiquity. (See note, p. 250.)

Let this suffice by way of introduction. My aim here is not to controvert, but only to expound a few salient philosophical standpoints, which, whether they be derived or original, are involved in the ethical views and methods advocated in the Pāli Canon.

CHAPTER II

DHAMMA AND ABHIDHAMMA

WHEN a Burmese, Singhalese or Siamese scholar, in matters religious and philosophical, discourses or writes, not in order to exhort or edify, but to analyze, define, classify and explain, he is said to be talking or writing not Dhamma, but Abhidhamma.

Now Dhamma, more familiar perhaps to us in its Vedic and Sanskrit form, *Dharma*, is an ancient Indian word, with the very wide meaning of Right, Good, Justice, Moral Law. The notion even came to be personified as a god among the gods. Etymologically, the word is of identical origin with our "form," the common Aryan root, according to Dr. Skeat, being 'dhar.' And 'dhar,' to quote further, means to support, sustain, maintain, hold, keep. We might therefore identify Dhamma with "good form," did this expression apply to higher matters than propriety or good taste. As signifying then "good form," raised, as mathematicians say, to a higher power, Dhamma implies that view or procedure which is, as we say, according to conscience, and constituting a more or less recognized standard, guiding rule, or norm. It is also translated by Paliyists as The Ideal, Truth, Law, Right, System or Doctrine, according to the context. Every religious or ethical teacher of ancient India had some "Dhamma" to propound. "What, sir,"—some teacher is now and again recorded as asking the Buddha—"is your Dhamma by which you so train your disciples, that they, having found consolation, recognize it as their ultimate support and fundamental principle of religious life?"

"Fundamental" is, by the commentator on this particular passage, paraphrased by ancient or pristine. And indeed this is never lost sight of in the Pāli books:—that the Buddha is expressing not only his own convictions, the fruit of intense effort and self-communing, but also something that was, and had in the infinite past been, and would ever be, objectively and constantly valid and true for any and every human society, nay, something that was cosmic law, eternal, necessary, omnipresent, whether discerned or not. And the function and hall-mark of a Buddha was not to devise, or create a new Dhamma, but to rediscover, recreate and revive that ancient norm. His it was to bring about its renascence as a cult in the lives, and apply it to the special needs, of his own age and its posterity. This, in words ascribed to him, is how the Buddha viewed his mission:—"As a man, brethren, wandering in the forest, in the mountain jungle, might see an ancient path, an ancient road, trodden by men of an earlier age; and following it, might discover an ancient township, an ancient palace, the habitation of men of an earlier age, surrounded by park and grove and lotus-pool and walls, a delightful spot; and that man were to go back, and announce to the king or his minister: Behold, sir, and learn what I have seen! And, having told him, he were to invite the king to rebuild that city, and that city were to become anon flourishing and populous and wealthy once more:—Even so, brethren, have I seen an ancient Path, an ancient Road, trodden by Buddhas of a bygone age . . . the which having followed, I understand life, and its coming to be and its passing away. And thus understanding, I have declared the same to the fraternity and to the laity, so that the holy life flourishes and is spread abroad once more, well propagated among men."[1]

And thus of course says every great reformer: "In the beginning was the Word" . . . "The words that I speak are not mine." Confucius too follows the Christ and the Buddha:—"My work is to indicate rather than to originate."

Dhamma, then, is of the common ancient Indian stock of ideas, peculiar as a term to no creed, and only immensely heightened and deepened by the Buddhists. For to them, as

[1] *Sutta-Pit'aka*, *Samyutta-Nikāya*, "The City."

meaning the normal, necessary and eternal order and law of all moral or spiritual things, it stood *in place of a theodicy*, or cosmos created and carried on by a first and a final cause. Never for them a deity, it was the Necessity behind the god, to which Æschylus, at more or less the same epoch, was pointing in his "Prometheus." As gravitation exists, whether Newtons arise to discern its action or not, so for Buddhists does Dhamma exist and act, whether the current age bring forth a Buddha or not.

Let us leave the matter for the moment at that. I may seem to be loading the word with a heavier import than is given to it by Pāli scholars, for instance, than that given by Rhys Davids in *Buddhist India* (p. 292), where he likens it to that "good form," which a man of right feeling will judge he should at any moment conform to. But I am not proposing to supersede this purely ethical aspect of Dhamma at all. In the passage referred to, the writer is discussing the use of Dhamma in the Asokan Edicts, and "the way in which it came to be used as it was in India, in Asoka's time." This, he writes, is not "Law," which is frequently used for Dhamma. Here I am not concerned so much with the ethical aspect, as with that background of philosophical postulates which, uttered or unexpressed, lies at the back of our most solemn judgments about life and the whole of things. And just as our use of "law" may vary, from mere by-law to a natural sequence of the universe, so did the Buddhist Indian "in the street," for whom the Edicts were intended, and Buddhaghosa the scholar, differ in the significance which Dhamma could bear for them.

Dhamma, Tao, Anangkē (necessity), Agathon (Plato's "Good"):—these all, with various shades of meaning and emphasis, represent as many utmost fetches of the early human intellect to conceive an impersonal principle, or order of things prior to, and more constant than, the administrative deity representing it. To ask of the systems developing severally those four notions:—If there, who put it there?"—is to invert their point of view. It is contrary to Buddhism to see in Dhamma the expression of a prior Consciousness. Buddhism is content to trace in human consciousness the evolution of cosmic norm or Dhamma. Herein we have come on to a fundamental concept in Buddhist philosophy.

But if Dhamma is a term common to Indian thought, Abhidhamma seems to be a term exclusively used by Buddhists. And for them, Abhidhamma, meaning literally beyond, or ultra-Dhamma, covers all study of theory as such, and of logical method. Just as Aristotle found the term physics ready to hand, but was himself the involuntary cause, if not the actual circulator of the term metaphysics, so does the term Abhidhamma start with Buddhism. That is to say, with Indian culture when this was Buddhist. The earliest expression of this side of that culture as yet known to be extant, is contained in the seven books of the Pāli Pitaka called the Abhidhamma-Pitaka. (Other seven books on Abhidhamma are those of the Sarvāstivādins —a school that split off early from the original stem of Buddhism. These are preserved in Chinese translations. Their titles and matter are different, but in method and scope they appear, from the slender outline of them as yet published,[1] to be akin to the Pāli books. In the near future they will become more accessible to us.) These seven books show that their authors were conversant with a logic of terms and propositions, of definition and division, that is like and also unlike the methods we have inherited from the Greeks. And these books of applied logic and method, formed together probably with the oldest and cognate works of the Jain school, the basis of the elaborate logic of mediæval India. "The real founders of the mediæval logic," writes Professor Vidyabhusana, of Calcutta, "were the Buddhists." That logic "was almost entirely in the hands of the Jainas and Buddhists" (*Mediæval School of Indian Logic*), although in the more ancient Abhidhamma Pitaka we have the logic applied only, and not yet systematized in text-books.

[1] By Professor Takakusu, *Journal* Pāli Text Society, 1905.

In fact the somewhat superficial acquaintance with these curious old books, which is all that any of us in Europe can yet claim to have, would almost lead us to suppose that they themselves served to some extent as manuals of logical method.

To a certain extent they select from, and restate, doctrines contained in the doctrinal, or Sutta, Pitaka. Besides this they define terms, and formulate propositions to a greater degree of precision. They also investigate a vast number of cases where they apply their formulæ. I may not in these brief limits stay to illustrate, and will add only this:

In the Abhidhamma-Pitaka we see the Pegasus of Indian imagination working for the first time in harness. Nowhere as in India do we see human phantasy so elastic and exuberant, sporting in time, space, and the infinite; and nowhere else as in this Theravāda literature appears such determined effort, not wholly to crush all its airy notions, but to curb, regulate and systematize them. Pegasus is yoked, but he retains his iridescent wings. The gods are *as such* become of no account. But they persist as happy, reborn human beings, longer lived, but no less impermanent. Any one who had the grit to practise the system of intense rapt self-hypnotic contemplation called Jhāna, and was sufficiently pure in heart thereby to attain abhiññā, or supernormal insight, could for himself see beyond this one plane of life. Were there not many saintly men and women who had testified thereto? And what they had told and taught had to be exploited and regulated in all this body of terms and formulæ. Hence the Buddhist Indian, thinking in harness, is by no means so confined in range of positive materials as the modern European.

None the less, Abhidhamma was an instrument for regulating the mind. According to the greatest of the scholastic commentators of the fifth century A.D., Buddhaghosa, it was calculated to check those excesses in thought away from the norm, which were shown, by the Buddha, to lead to loss of mental balance, craziness, insanity. And this it was sought to carry out, first, by a thorough-going definition and determination of all terms used in doctrinal tenets. Hereby a mutual consistency of denotation and connotation was secured. Secondly, by enunciating those tenets in a fixed form, and co-ordinating them mutually, where desirable. Thirdly, by reducing all possible heterodox positions to an absurdity. Fourthly,—and herein lies the chief, not to say the only direction in which the Abhidhamma-Pitaka has positively contributed to early Buddhist philosophy—by a study of the most general relations conceivable among phenomena. These are reckoned as twenty-four in number, some of which we should subsume, or include under others, perhaps because in English dress their real meaning is not always clear. Here are some of them :—

A phenomenon may be related to another by way of " condition, object, influence, co-existence, contiguity, reciprocity, succession," . . . and so on.

And all this body of mental discipline, be it remembered, was taught without books. The style of the books themselves never lets us forget it, and they make shockingly bad *reading* in consequence. Often, the only way used to aid the burdened memory is an orderly but endless repetition of a verbal framework, wherein only one term of a series is varied at a time. We may smile and yawn over the results, and we may talk pityingly of *epigonoi* and scholastic pedantry. Yet the aims were lofty, and the execution, in the absence of visible registering apparatus, extraordinary. I am even tempted to wonder how far the exaggeration of the Indian temperament and the temperance of the Greek temperament were due to the absence and presence respectively, during the florescence of each, of the fully *written* thought.

Let us agree to see in Abhidhamma, both in the Pitaka so-called and out of it, Buddhist mental and moral science, based on the Dhamma of the Pāli Pitakas, and go on to consider it as tradition. Discounting the changed skies above it, for as we saw, the tradition of Dhamma and Abhidhamma is an exile, it may rank among the most venerable survivals of early culture. Assuming that Gotama Buddha died in the fifth century, B.C., and that the Canon started, grew, and finally took its present shape during the course of the two following centuries, we see, in that Canon and the South Asian literature that has accumulated round it, a continuous doctrinal succession, first oral, then both oral and literary, of approximately 2,200 years, if not more. More perhaps in the case of parts of the first two Pitakas; parts of the Sutta-Pitaka and the Abhidhamma-Pitaka being certainly not so old. We shall not, therefore, be very wide of the mark if we consider the unification of Indian learning under Buddhism to be not many decades removed from the unification of Greek learning under Aristotle.

Now there is this salient difference in the continuity of Buddhist Abhidhamma as compared with that of Graeco-Christian philosophy; namely, that for us the thoughts of Plato, Aristotle, and their forerunners run alongside the current of our Christian doctrine like two streams that will not wholly mingle. They have been handed down partly by the Christian Church, partly in spite of its earlier efforts. The contentions in the early Christian Church as to how far Greek philosophy might wisely be annexed and taught, form interesting matter for the historian.

But for Buddhists, the method called Abhidhamma has sprung from the very tree itself of the Dhamma. It is for them of no pagan stock, admitted at first on sufferance by the doctors of a faith come otherwhence to birth and power. To realize the unity in the tradition of the Theras, we must try to conceive the vista that Christian philosophy would present, could we transpose the first centuries Anno Domini and the last centuries preceding them,—could we make Socrates and Plato to have been trained at the feet of St. Peter or St. Paul, or could we make a Christian Abhidhammika of Aristotle. Not then would the Christian poet, who called him "Master of them that know," have consigned his spirit to a neutral after-world in Limbo's tremulous air for having, all unknowing, "not rightly worshipped God." (Dante's *Inferno*, c. iv.)

Abhidhamma has, as we know, long ceased to be taught in the Palestine or Holy Land of Buddhism. Of the chief centres where it was successively taught, Jetăvănă's site lies revealed in utter ruin, and over Nālandā's university, swept away by fire and sword, the little ploughs scratch the obliterating soil. But the torch of the Theras, handed on by missionary ardour to centres of civilization in Ceylon and Further India, has furnished a fire from those Indian mother-altars that has never become extinct. In the vihāras of Ceylon, Siam and Burma, the Pāli Canon is and has been taught as authoritative from its introduction till now. And it is remarkable, when we compare palm-leaf Pāli MSS., written in the different characters of each of these countries, to see how relatively few, and especially how doctrinally negligeable are the mutual discrepancies in the text. To the doctrines as set forth in the Canon, the mediæval and modern works on Abhidhamma lines loyally and piously adhere.

This was perhaps only to be expected, since all greatly divergent thought had severed itself early from the parent stock. On the other hand, it must be remembered that this residual unity of tradition has been maintained without any restriction affecting liberty or life imposed by a presiding authority. Could any other surviving tradition of so long standing say as much ?

But this continuous orthodoxy has by no means excluded a quietly evolving vitality. It has resembled, not the dead waters of a canal, but the slow and gentle meandering of a river of the plains. Our knowledge of Abhidhamma literature is as yet deplorably deficient. But we know enough at least of the older portion of it to see a considerable advance in analytic power. Of the three works extant known to be prio to, because quoted by, Buddhaghosa—prior, that is, to the fifth century A.D., the one accessible to English readers is "The Questions of King Milinda." In the learned Nāgasena's replies, even though these are adapted to the relatively untrained intelligence of the King, we note a marked psychological progress, and a fine deftness of philosophical exposition. To this we may return. The psychology in the works of Buddhaghosa himself shows a still more noteworthy evolution.

By his time the philosophical culture of Buddhist India was expressing itself in Sanskrit. In the literature of that culture there is ample testimony, in such works as survive, to reveal developments in logic and in metaphysic. But Buddhaghosa belonged to the Pāli tradition of the Theravādins, and wrote in Ceylon. And in making accessible the works of him and his successors, much work yet remains to be done. The brief summary of philosophy called *A Compendium of Abhidhamma*, which has for many centuries, together with a great accretion of commentarial works, formed the nucleus of instruction in southern Buddhist centres till the present day, shows that attempts at philosophical synthesis were ever in progress, even though no great constructive intellect made any striking departure. In the present decade the philosophic world of the Burmese monasteries is much engaged by the innovations in traditional lines of thought put forward by the Thera, Ledi Sadaw (*i.e.*, Professor Ledi).

Better knowledge of mediæval and modern Buddhist literature may show that the different countries cultivating it—Ceylon, Burma, Siam, to go no further—may, by national differences in culture, diction and environment, have each acquired specific characteristics of doctrine. Such divergence will, however, have been held in check, first, by the carefully preserved unity in the canonical literature, secondly, by the great work of Buddhaghosa, whose "Way of Purity" (soon to become accessible to English readers) and commentaries, have served as a causeway of orthodoxy; thirdly, by the practice, similar to that which obtained among ourselves in the Middle Ages even more than now, of Buddhist students internationalizing their resorts of learning. As Latin was our *lingua franca* among travelling scholars, so has Pāli ever been theirs. Pāli is still the language in which most Abhidhamma books are written. And a better acquaintance, I repeat, with those books, old and new, will reveal such variation, due to race and environment, as these checks have not sufficed to prevent.

No doubt, on the other hand, a tradition which has lived so long immune from shocks and strains from without, let alone from serious schisms from within, is scarcely one that can be expected to evolve and expand in adequate response to the progressive birth-throes of the human mind. Its long slumber as to any further missionizing efforts of its own, its long immunity from contact with alien thought, must involve it in some experiences of Rip van Winkle's, when the sleeper comes forth. We shall expect to find, side by side with those great traits that made early

Buddhism immortal, the clinging nimbus of child-like and uncritical fancies and beliefs. We do find them both in the literature of the past and in the current tradition. But the fact that the long life-span of Buddhism presents this composite figure of features and nimbus, detracts not an iota from its interest for us—its interest for the history of philosophy and its interest for the thinkers who are making the philosophy of to-morrow.

For consider a moment the exceeding great historical interest that lies in the fact and nature of an ancient unbroken tradition. We of Europe move along the orbit of a philosophical tradition that we like to trace back some twenty-five centuries to Thales, mid-way between east and west. This we call " the " Greek philosophical tradition. But it has not only assimilated streams from non-Hellenistic sources ; it is the fittest survivor among many wrecks, as are no doubt all other traditions. " Fittest " perhaps because it throve more easily than others, amid the varying myths and conventions of the social soil it grew upon.

Among those wrecks of thought, we may count the philosophic syntheses of Herakleitus, and of Leukippus and Demokritus. Their works have perished. Their thoughts were not all drowned, but they were, so to speak, hauled out of the sea on to the decks of the Academic and Stoan Armadas. In plain words, they live for us chiefly because Plato and Aristotle quoted them, as good stimulators for argument and refutation. Even if the sand-buried ruins of Egyptian villas had revealed to us anything so precious as the great Diakosmos by Demokritus, or the untitled discourses of Herakleitus, we should have but the beginnings of that whereof some crumbs only have survived. We should have no consecutive tradition.

But in the Dhamma we have implicit from the first, and, in Abhidhamma teaching we have, made gradually explicit, a synthesis on all fours with the universal flux of Herakleitus and with Demokritus's theory of natural causation. Hence the enhanced degree of interest for us in the Buddhist philosophical tradition as maintained by the Theravāda. It is not only of a relatively pure and independent pedigree; it is also the Eastern counterpart of certain notable syntheses which, originating between East and West, were never, in the West, made the headstone of the corner in philosophy's temple. Modern science, which now sways philosophy to and fro, is no doubt in line with the thought of both Herakleitus and Demokritus, and is their ultimate vindicator. But science, bent on present and future vision, leaves her tradition to the care of the historical philosopher. He has to explain how she arose from a soil which had suffered Demokritus's works to perish, while in Buddhist soil, with the exception of a notable medical and psychological culture, she failed to grow.

CHAPTER III

THE NORM AS THEORY OF NO SOUL

We have so far gained some idea of the history and scope of that Pāli Buddhism to a limited study of which these pages are confined. We must now come to closer grips with those inductions and ideals in this Pāli Buddhism, which will one day, despite the slenderly based criticism that would rob them of all originality, be considered as a positive contribution to the history of philosophy.

It was asserted in the preceding chapter, that Dhamma (or Norm) implied, for the philosophical Buddhist, an impersonal eternal order of things, according to which all things, animate and inanimate, gods included, lived, moved and had their being. This is not the Buddhist's usual way of describing it. Nevertheless in the oldest books the conviction is there as a latent, undefined but most vital postulate, and is borne in upon us as we read. We find, namely, (1) a universe of many worlds, without first cause, going on from everlasting to everlasting, by alternating integration and disintegration; (2) this cosmic procedure as orderly, both as to physical, psychical and moral nature; (3) no caprice, chance or chaos existing anywhere in this cosmos.

When Buddhist-Indian thought had become sufficiently analytic and self-conscious to distinguish and formulate its philosophical postulates, it analyzed the implications of the term Dhamma. We know this analysis through the pen of Buddhaghosa, who does not claim originality in the matter. Dhamma, he wrote,[1] signifies (1) The Doctrine, as a verbal, or literary composition to be learnt and mastered (*pariyatti*). (2) Condition or cause (*hetu*). This is illustrated by the quotation: "Dhamma-analysis is knowledge concerning conditions"[2] (3) Right, or righteousness. This is illustrated by the verse:

> Not of the like result are right and wrong (*dhamma, a-dhamma*),
> Wrong leads to baleful, right, to happy doom.[3]

(4) phenomenon. The Pāli word here used is *nissatta-nijjīvatā*, *i.e.*, non-entity or non-substrate, and *non-soul-ness*. This is illustrated elsewhere by the quotations: "When mental phenomena arise in consciousness." "He contemplating the nature of phenomena."[4]

In this fourfold explication of the term

[1] Commentary on the *Dhamma-Sangani*; also that on the *Dhammapada*. The identity of the author of the latter work with Buddhaghosa is doubtful.

[2] *Vibhanga* (Abhidhamma-Pitaka).

[3] *Psalms of the Brethren* (Sutta-Pitaka).

[4] *Psychological Ethics*, 33 [121]; *Majjhima-Nikāya*, i. 61.

Dhamma we may see the whole of Theravāda Buddhist philosophy in a nutshell. In the beloved person of the Buddha were enshrined all that Divine Presences, wisdom stooping from on high, transcendent love and power mighty and willing to save, the secret of genius knowing and drawing the hearts of men, the ideal Superman, have availed and wrought for humanity in other creeds. In the institution of an organized Fraternity and a loyal Laity—the Order giving, the Laity giving also, but believing it received yet more than it gave—the slow evolution of solidarity took the best shape practicable at the time. Thirdly and lastly, the notion of Dhamma included, and stood for, the fact and growth of ideas, fruit of the mind and yet condition and fashioner of minds; interpreted and transmitted by men, and yet that wherein and whereby they "lived and moved and had their being." And insight into Dhamma, we read in the Sutta-Pitaka, meant the discernment of an eternal, orderly, conditioned sequence of things, the which, when thoroughly grasped, swept out of a man's thoughts all speculation on the beginning of life or its ultimate end, or on its present nature as entity or soul.[1]

Let us now beat out a little more fully each of these four aspects of the word Dhamma, and thereby test the statement that they give us together the kernel of Buddhism.

[1] *Samyutta-Nikāya*, ii. 25-27, 60.

And let us take the last aspect first, namely, that *Dhamma* might stand for *phenomenon*, especially anything that we say is mental object, or state of mind. How does it belong to the essence of Buddhist thought to emphasize the fact that in mental states we have phenomena, and not anything behind phenomena, such as soul or ego, or substance? For Buddhist thought is very emphatic indeed about it, and makes this rejection of a something which, as the subject of mental states, does not come and go with them, but persists unchanging and unending, its first and last philosophic denial. So much so, that it has been accused of being simply a system of negation, without any positive structure whatever.

Quotations might be multiplied by the dozen, but I give one or two that best represent the mass of such rejections of the substantialist position. To Vaj'ĭrā, a Sister of the Order, these verses are ascribed :—

Māra.

Who hath this being (*satta*) fashionèd ? Where is
The maker of this being ? Whence hath it sprung ?
Where doth this being cease and pass away ?

Vajirā.

" Being ? " Why dost thou harp upon that word ?
'Mong false opinions, Māra, art thou strayed.
This a mere bundle of formations is.
Therefrom no " being " mayest thou obtain,
For e'en as, when the factors are arranged,
By the word " chariot " is the product known,

> So doth our usage covenant to say
> "A being" when the Aggregates are there.[1]

Again Ānanda, the companion of the Buddha, asks him: "What is meant, lord, by the phrase, 'the world is empty?'" "That it is empty, Ānanda, of a self, or of anything of the nature of a self. And what is it that is thus empty? The five seats of the five senses, and the mind, and the feeling that is related to mind:—all these are void of a self or of anything that is self-like."[2]

Again to the listening brethren or bhikkhus:—"Since neither self nor aught belonging to self, brethren, can really and truly exist, the view which holds that this [I] who am 'world,' who am 'self,' shall hereafter live permanent, persisting, eternal, unchanging, yea, abide eternally: is not this utterly and entirely a foolish doctrine?"[3]

This denial of a permanent self or soul (*attā*) in any living being whatever was extended, logically enough, to the whole hierarchy of gods or superhuman beings, wherewith the Indian heavens, not to say earth and all regions, are so liberally populated. All were "living creatures," and life in all its manifestations, in the very nature of it, was impermanent and subject to change and to suffering. Thus we

[1] *Psalms of the Sisters*, p. 190.

[2] *Samyutta-Nikāya*, iv. 54. [Aggregates or groups: constituents, mental and bodily, of a person.]

[3] *Majjhima-Nikāya* (Sutta-Pitaka), i. 138.

read in the "Lion" Sutta[1] how, in their long, long span of pleasant being, the gods forget this, till at length a Buddha arises in the world. "And just as the king of beasts at eventide comes forth from his lair and roars, so that all the beasts tremble and hide, so does he proclaim the Norm to gods and to men, how all matter and all mind recombines and dissolves again. Thereat the gods hear and in anguish exclaim: Alas! we who fancied ourselves permanent, stable, eternal, we are confined by an individuality that is impermanent, unstable, temporary!"

Again, a special case of this illusion being dispelled is given in the legend-sutta of the Brahma-god Băkă, who appears to the Buddha and declares the Brahma-heaven to be permanent, etc., without birth, decay, or decease, and that beyond it is no salvation. The Buddha replies, that only because of his ignorance can Băkă affirm his heaven to be eternal, absolute, free from the law of impermanence, or affording ultimate salvation.[2]

It will be seen that there is no attempt here, in denying the absolute in all deity, to deny also that gods exist. That they existed was taken for granted. They lived longer and more pleasantly, they had superior, less limited organisms, and better powers of locomotion. But they existed, law-governed, like mankind, that is to say, the world-order fulfilled itself in them; they did not create it,

[1] *Samyutta-Nikāya*, iii. 85. [2] *Op. cit.* i. 142.

nor could they destroy it, or interfere with it. It is true that we read of misdeeds of men affecting nature locally, *e.g.*, in the supply of rain, withheld by nature spirits. But they are not in any way lords and governors to be prayed to and propitiated. The good Buddhist knew that he as such had nothing to fear from them. And to-day, though they may no longer be held to flit from heaven to earth, " as it were a strong man darting out his arm," or throng around as when a Buddha preaches the Norm, still do they exist for any orthodox Buddhist. Why limit an infinite universe to humanity? he would say. So much then, and so little is there of atheism in his creed.

Neither had it any quarrel with the convenient, not to say necessary notion whereby we each of us speak of, and picture ourselves as " I," or a self (*attā*). " The self reproaches the self " is the Pāli idiom for a troubled conscience. And " the taming of self," " the right poising of the self," and " self-advantage " are all terms of Buddhist ethics. All such, as the Commentator remarks, are mere conventions of language. True, the testimony of normal consciousness is to a unity. Mental science tends, however, as we know, to support the Buddhist position. Experience, it says, shows that the unity often by no means works as such. Pathology tells us a good deal more to the same effect. The unity is not only of factors that are perpetually changing, and often fail to co-operate harmoniously, but is liable to be split up into two, or even three unities of consciousness. Still, normally each of us is a unified "bundle of formations," as Sister Vajirā said. And the "bundle" must have its verbal sign. Buddhist Abhidhamma fell in with this popular usage, but guarded itself in so doing. So Buddhaghosa, commenting on the Pitaka phrase :—"included in the concrete personality" (literally self-state), says : "from the foolish public's notion that 'this is *my self*,' body and mind are called self-state."

But the moment that language serves, not merely, as here, to signify the temporary bundle in man or god, but to uphold animistic and absolutist beliefs, emphatic repudiation of the word "self" or "soul" appears. In other words, whenever the word *attā* implies that in the temporary bundle is a mysterious little being, which uses the changing body as a shell, coming at or before birth, and flitting away at death, itself unchanged, eternal, above the laws of nature, then does the word become the sign of the worst of errors. The conception of the inner sprite or double is universal in folk-beliefs, and in this respect we speak of such conceptions as animistic. When this inner mannikin is still further sublimated, and all that remains is the concept of it as the real being, or underlying substance or substrate, to which all the qualities or attributes of an individual are said to belong, and so to become a unity, we speak of such conceptions as absolutistic. The English term in this case is usually changed from soul to self, or ego. But, in the latter case, the super-phenomenal self or ego must of course be understood, and not the mere mark for the "bundle."

Now Buddhist philosophy, in repudiating both animistic soul and absolutistic self, was aimed at a special shape assumed by such theories in India. This was an aspect of both which sought to satisfy at once, (1) the child-like questioning answered by animism, (2) the logic which sees in all objects first the completed whole and then the factors, and (3) man's veneration for the creative genius and synthetic ideas of man. All this was comprised in the Indian cult of the universal self, or soul, conceived, not only, or so much, as external to man while immanent in the universe, but as immanent in man, and as man's own and very self. This was the cult of the Ātman (Sanskrit for *attā*), and we may speak of it as Ātmanism.

In the oldest Indian hymns, the Rig-Veda, the wind is called the *ātman* or breath of Văruṇă, who is the nearest approach we there find to a personification of the idea of cosmic order. But breath came to be identified with deity, and was also considered as a symptom of soul within. So, analogously to the Christian idea of *pneuma*, which came to mean both breath and spirit, the concept of *ātman* grew, till it was used interchangeably with Brahman, the cosmic principle pervading the universe, and also with the human *prāna* (breath) or soul. On its more esoteric, mystical, devotional side, as revealed in the works now committed to writing, and called Upănishăds,[1] this cult of the Ātman may, nay, must be taken into account, if we are to understand the strength of the Buddhist protest, and the peculiar logic of its attack. Judging by the descriptions given in the Pitakas, the age teemed with animistic superstition, metaphysical dogmas on the soul and mysticism. But it is the Ātmanist position against which the Buddhist argument is drawn up, as we shall presently see.

There is no attack worth mentioning made by Buddhism on the notion of Brahman, the impersonal principle of cosmic life and order. As a personal deity, Brahmā is treated as a leading *deva* among *devas*, but one whose approval or displeasure matters nothing to man's salvation. His eminence is handled with irony, when the monopoly of omniscience is claimed for him.[2] And the devotional exercises, which were currently believed to aid in bringing about after-life in his heaven, were adopted in Buddhism, less for this purpose, which the Buddha called "low," than to forward emancipation of heart. (See p. 218 f.)

[1] *Sacred Books of the East*, vols. I., XV.

[2] *Dialogues of the Buddha*, i. 280 ff.

But when that cosmic principle is considered not only as world-soul, but as the very soul of Me, the realization of which was held as the supreme and saving truth,—then Buddhism joins issue and fights without compromise.

"In the beginning," runs an old Upanishad,[1] "the world was only soul, in the shape of a man. . . . He sent forth worlds. . . . If a man understands the Self saying, 'I am He' . . . he indeed is the creator. . . his is the world, and he is the world itself . . if a man clearly beholds this Self as God, and as the lord of all that is and that will be, then he is no more afraid."

"Void is the world," rejoins the Buddhist, "of self, or of aught of that nature." If it is contended that, by the context to this passage, quoted above (p. 52), only the phenomenal world of sense-perception is stated to be meant, we should inevitably come elsewhere on passages conceding (or indeed insisting on) the existence of a soul not immanent in, but transcending that phenomenal world. *What we find* is (*a*) the affirmation that "all the religious world who consider the soul as variously bestowed, consider it to be the five constituents of personality (*khandha's*) or some one of them,"[2] (*b*) consistent and constant negation that the soul is "in," or associated with any of the five.

It is this beholding self as god, this seeing in the phenomenal "bundle" the superpheno-

[1] *Brihadāranyaka-Ūp.* [2] *Samyutta-Nikāya,* iii. 46.

menal or absolute, to which the Buddhist takes exception. The Ātman was "eternal," "immortal," "free from decay, death and sorrow," "real." Well then, said the Buddhist, every object, and every means of knowing objects—all, in fact, is impermanent, you will admit. Now that which is impermanent is liable to change and suffering, and is not free, *i.e.*, it is bound by its law-governed phenomenal nature. Is it then fit to say of any such object or subject; it is for me Ātman; it is Ego or the soul of me? This is the standard staple form of argument used in a great number of Pitaka Suttas. And if we read into the words, soul, self, ego the tremendous import attached to them in the preceding Upanishad citations. . . . "I (Ego) am (world-) Ātman" . . . "beholds this Self as God" . . . we realize that a dogmatic mysticism so abnormal was bound to evoke a religious and philosophical recoil. The protest of Buddhism, viewed thus in its local context, appears natural and inevitable, rather than captious or unreasonable.

But the mystical climax of soul-cult in Ātmanism was by no means the only form of it with which Buddhism contended. As an extreme form of soul-dogma it was well known (many of the Theras were lapsed Brahmins). But the general contention was wider. The forms of soul-dogma stated in the Pitakas consist in a number of mutually controversial speculations as to the nature and destiny of the self or soul, considered under aspects that are not absolute or divine, and which are therefore nearer to similar speculations in European metaphysic, *e.g.*, that the self or soul is finite, or infinite, is material or immaterial, happy or miserable after death, self-made or made by another, eternal or not eternal. These various hypotheses are catalogued several times in the Sutta-Pitaka,[1] or are singly dealt with,[2] as so many futile, unprofitable forms of intellectual dalliance. One feature in which they differ from Western theories, is that we never meet with hypotheses respecting "souls" or "selves," and their inter-relations, as is the case, for instance, in Leibnitz's theory of monads. They are concerned with "soul."

Speculation of this sort is met with chiefly in the mouths of members of itinerant religious fraternities, of whom there were many when Buddhism arose. They foregathered in park and meeting-hall, discussing such themes with much free speech, seeking truth and salvation in their own way. But it was a strained, unhealthy condition of thought, and the inevitable reaction against all this sort of animistic speculation, whether pantheistic or individualistic, was constituted by the standpoint taken up by one such itinerant fraternity, to wit that of the Sākya-sons, as they were called, or as we say, the Buddhists.

1 *E.g. Dialogues of the Buddha*, i. 41-53.

2 *E.g.* Majjhima-Nikāya, ii. 32-7.

Not less, and to a very conscious degree, was Buddhism a protest against a certain variety of scepticism current at the time. But with this we shall better be able to deal when engaged on its philosophy of causation. Here I wish to dwell on the very definite and remarkable impress given to their religion and philosophy precisely in consequence of, and as a weapon against, this state of overwrought metaphysical speculation. I refer to the science of mind, or psychology, which the Buddhist movement initiated, and which Buddhist culture subsequently developed. In this respect, the Buddhists are the true Eastern compeers of Aristotle and Western psychology, and the day will come when their analysis of mind will rank, in the history of psychology, and from a universal standpoint, equal in achievement with that of the Greeks, and indeed of Europe generally, up to the time when psycho-physiology was introduced.

This mental analysis is quite unmythological and scientific. The older, pre-Buddhistic Upanishads contain fine germs of psychological insight, shadowy outlines of a theory of sense-perception in particular. But the tone is child-like and poetical; the utterances are sporadic aphorisms. Moon and gods and demons are ever at hand as an explanation of functions not investigated. There is a lack of sobriety. The Pitakas, on the other hand, not only in Abhidhamma catechism, but even in the doctrinal discourses and poems of the Suttas, give us sober and prosaic *description of what they find* obtaining in mental processes. Of figures, similes and analogies there is no lack, but these are consciously and discreetly used in order to illustrate. Fancies are not treated as perceptions. The five modes of sense, for instance, are compared to doors, to the sea, to a field, to an empty village (without headman or soul), when ethical teaching is thereby rendered more graphic. But when knowing by way of sense has to be *analyzed,* we then get simply the results of observation and inference. "Given eye and visible object, visual consciousness arises; the conjunction of the three is 'contact,' whereby conditioned, arises feeling, whereby conditioned, arises perception, etc."[1] Again: "What is the sense of hearing? The ear, that is, the sentient organ, derived from the four elements, forming part of the person (self-state), invisible and reacting, whereby one has heard, hears, will, or may hear sounds invisible and impinging . . . which itself impinges on sounds, and depending on which ear and sound, audible contact arises . . . this is the sense, the constituent element, the faculty of hearing."[2] In the later book, *Milinda,* the teacher illustrates the collision of sense and object by two butting rams, and by clashing

[1] *Majjhima-Nikāya*, i. 111.

[2] *Psychological Ethics,* 178.

cymbals. But he taught his royal pupil after a popular fashion.

It may be objected that this is no explanation, only description. But science is mainly description, in so far as it is not experimental, a description of the particular case in terms of a general case, either of object or process. And to start with description is a better basis for the advance of knowledge, than to block the path of inference and synthesis by invoking transcendental agencies.

Such a basis, these early and archaic, but sincere and earnest attempts at analysis is proved to be for the expanding culture of the succeeding centuries. The *Milinda* contains many developments in mental science, notably in a theory of association, and an analysis of memory.[1] Similes are again used, for the king's intelligence has to be reckoned with, that is, one without technical training in such matters. But they are used strictly to illustrate, and, by illustrating, to extend the conception of natural law to the working of the mind, and to dispel the idea of any animistic agencies.[2]

Yet more marked is the psychological advance met with in the works of Buddhaghosa. From these we can see that the introspective analysis of mental processes had been carried far. As among ourselves, it is the process of coming to know by way of

[1] *Questions of King Milinda*, i. 37, 89, 122.

[2] *Cf.* below, p.

sense that has proved most amenable to investigation. The result is a more detailed resolution into factors than European psychology can show. Very briefly stated, every conscious act of sense-perception (*e.g.* the hearing of a bell, the sight of a person entering the room), was resolved into these successive moments: (1) vibrations in sub-consciousness; (2) adverting of the " doors " of sense; (3) the sense-impression; (4) the door of mind receiving; (5) examining; (6) determining (the nature of 3); (7) full cognition; (8) retention. All of which might occupy a quite infinitesimal fraction of time.

But detailed inquiry of this kind belongs to the history of psychology. The salient feature in it for our present purpose is the fact that, for Buddhist thought, from the start, psychological insight is an integral part of philosophical, nay, of religious insight. It started not with the external universe, and its first or final cause, but with the heart of man, sentient and desiring. " In this fathom-long conscious *be-minded* body, I declare the world to be, and the uprising of the world, and the ceasing of the world, and the course leading to that cessation."[1] Training in mental analysis was considered essential both as ethical discipline, and as clearing the way for sound philosophy.

This emphasis on introspective alertness has been deprecated both by (modern) Mahā-

[1] *Samyutta-Nikāya*, i. 62; *Anguttara-Nikāya*, ii. 48.

Yānists and by non-Buddhists, hence it is worth while to pause over it, not in an apologetic or contrary spirit, but to understand it. The cities and villages of North-East India no doubt comprised not only considerable ethnical variety—Aryan, Dravidian, Kolarian—but as many varieties of temperament as other populous centres. But, judging by early Buddhist literature, the prevalent type seems to have been of a nervous, eager, high-strung, emotional nature, passionate and pleasure-seeking in disposition, swiftly elated or depressed, open and amenable to argument, capable of whole-hearted devotion and of strenuous effort. To these impulsive, quick-hearted children of the sun, impressions on their swift and delicate sense were interesting and absorbing chiefly as *feeling*, pleasant, painful or neutral. The Suttas emphasize this aspect of experience as likely to appeal to listeners—"There are sights, sounds, touches . . . apprehensible by this or that sense, which are wished-for, agreeable, delightful, fascinating, involving sensuous satisfaction, and exciting passionate longing." We hear in fact no less often about *how* sense affected, than about *what* is told.

Together with such testimony to much exuberance in response to sensuous impressions, we learn also that the means for gratifying sensuous and æsthetic impulse and taste were very numerous. Arts ministering to eye and ear were cultivated; the ravishing effect of music is especially mentioned. Odours exercised a powerful effect. Skin-sensibility was flattered by bath, massage and shampoo. Food and drinks were refined to suit the epicure. Dancing and sports were staple amusements.

And where conscious reaction is largely sensuous and emotional, the experience is referred intensively to the subject or self, more than it is referred extensively or externally to the object.

All serious departures in religion and ethics have of course striven to cope with the tendency to let life be swallowed up in the quest of sensuous gratification. And among the remedies sought have been pure askesis, or the suppression to the utmost limit consistent with life of the channels of sense-impression, and again the cultivation of the object-world apart from sense-pleasure, namely, in relation to ethical and intellectual interests. A third course is so to study and regulate the subject-world, or mind, that we can regard it as one object among other objects. Now the extent to which the Buddhists initiated and developed this third course is a notable and practically unique feature in their religious culture.

From the outset they deliberately and explicitly rejected asceticism. In the first sermon ascribed to the Buddha, he declared his method to be a middle way between asceticism and self-indulgence. Again, he is said, in another Sutta, to have asked the pupil of a Brahmin teacher, whether and how Pārāsariya taught a method of disciplining sense? "Yes," was the reply, "one does not see sights with the eyes, nor hear sounds with the ear. This is his method." "On that system," rejoins the Buddha, "the blind and the deaf have their senses the best under control." He proceeded to show how his method differs. Namely, sense-impressions are to be consciously discriminated psychologically, and then ethically appraised as inferior to disinterestedness or indifference. Thus cognitive and analytic, man is to be able to dictate to his own feelings. And thus, by learning habitually to break up the complex web of conscious experience, the Buddhist sought to gain a dual vantage-point: control over sense and impulse on the one hand, and, on the other, insight into the compound and conditioned nature of that which *seemed* to be a unitary Ego, or subject of conscious experience.

So much was this method felt and realized by its followers to be really of the essence of the doctrine, that it served both to define that doctrine and to betray its teacher. Thus, in the Sutta called *Analysis of Elements*" (*Majjhima-Nikāya*, No. 140), we read of the Buddha lodging for a night at the Potter's House in Rājagaha (Rājgir in Behar), who explains that he has already a lodger, a friar of noble rank. This was Pukkusāti, ex-King of Taxila in Kashmir, who, according to the commentarial tradition, had abdicated and left the world, in consequence of having learnt the Buddhist doctrines. These had been sent him, inscribed on a golden tablet, by his friend, King Bimbisāra, whose residence was at Rājagaha. The Buddha apologized: " If it be not disagreeable to you, brother, let us lodge one night together." The other consented, addressing the strange friar by the appellation, used between religious brethren, of *āvuso*. After each, sitting cross-legged, had meditated part of the night, the Buddha, noting the other's serene demeanour, asked him concerning his motive for leaving the lay-world, his teacher and his " Dhamma " ? Pukkusāti confesses that it was the Exalted One, Gotama of the Sākyas, whose Dhamma had so moved him." " Where, bhikkhu, is now that Gotama ? " " In the north country, friend, at Sāvatthī." " Have you seen him ? If you saw him, would you know him ? " " Nay, friend, if I saw him, I should not know him." " Listen, bhikkhu, I will teach you Dhamma." " So be it, friend." And the Buddha began with a summary. Man consisted of six constituent elements (earth, *i.e.*, extended element, water, heat, air, space and consciousness); he had six fields of contact with the external world (mind being the sixth); in eighteen ways he was affected by that world; and there is a fourfold platform, whereon if he stand, the surgings of fancy make no headway, and he is fit to be called sage and saint. That platform is (1) Ariyan[1] insight, *i.e.*, knowledge how to destroy all sorrow; (2) Ariyan truth or Nibbāna (*i.e.*, Nirvana); (3) Ariyan resignation, namely, of all conditions leading to rebirth; (4) Ariyan peace, *i.e.*, the tranquillization of lust, hate and illusion. These heads are then briefly developed, the "surgings of fancy" being credulous theorizing about one's present and future self or identity.

As he ceased, Pukkusāti, overcome with emotion, as he realized: "I have found the Master! I have found the Perfectly Enlightened One!" fell at the teacher's feet, beseeching forgiveness for having spoken as to an equal.

This simple episode, with the touching suggestion of the disciple's growing wonder, his "heart burning within him while he spake," ought to serve as a test case of utterances that were definitely and unmistakably what we now call Buddhist. And those utterances start with analysis of concrete personality and sense-cognition.

Again, the doctrine is sometimes defined as a body of analyses, in the phrase "taught me the Dhamma: *khandhâyatana-dhātuyo*";

[1] "Ariyan" conveyed to Buddhists much what our "Christian" does to us. Originally a racial term, it had come to mean "noble, gentle," and specifically, "elect in the Dhamma." To distinguish this derived meaning, I retain the Indian spelling (with *i*).

i.e., factors, bodily and mental (*khandhā*), sense-organs and objects (*āyatana*), and elements (*dhātuyo*). We should not imagine that a doctrine so described could arouse much emotion. Yet the Buddha's disciples are recorded as weaving this phrase, when describing how they had found light, into grateful verse. Thus Vangīsa, a distinguished Thera and poet, on his conversion :—

Mere strolling poets we of old ; we roamed
From town and village on to town again.
Then saw we Him, the Buddha, and in us
Rose up full trust. The Norm He taught to me :—
The factors, organs, bases of this self.[1]

So, too, the Sisters or nuns in their verses :—

Then She to this poor Bhikkhunī drew near,
Who was my foster-mother in the faith.
She taught to me the Norm, wherein I learnt
The factors, organs, bases of this self,
Impermanent compound. Hearing her words,
Beside her I sat down to meditate.[2]

Finally a very early appellation by which the Buddhists were known was that of Vibhajja-vādins, or Analytic School. And a testimony to the deep-seated and long-lived bent, imparted to the doctrine by the prominence given to analysis, may be seen in the journal of Yuan Chwang, the Chinese pilgrim mentioned above (p. 26). He found public debates being held near Peshawer, in Kashmir, on what the translator renders as " the nature

[1] *Samyutta-Nikāya*, i. 196.
[2] *Psalms of the Sisters*, xxx., xxxviii.

of the sense-perceptions." Even to the present day, the Theravādin school has ever remained predominantly analytical, and, in its analysis, predominantly psychological.

The product of this scientific habit of mind with which we are now most familiar, is the doctrine of the Five Khandhas or Aggregates or Groups. Into these five the concrete person or living organism was divided. Where we say soul and body, body, mind and spirit, mind and body, matter and mind, the Buddhists, from the inception of the movement, said the five *khandha's* (Sanskrit, *skandha's*). The division, whether originally Buddhist or not, is fairly unwieldy, and is, in scheme and in name, not a very happy essay in analysis. For the Buddhist standpoint, from which every " thing " is no static quantity, but a *happening*, or continual becoming, aggregate is not very helpful. The commentator, however, insists on " heap " (*rāsi*) as the meaning. Again, as a mental classification, the division is redundant. Thus of the five aggregates, one is the material factor, or body ; the other four are feeling (pleasure, pain, neutral feeling), perception (recognizing and naming), *sankhāra's* or the fifty other mental accompaniments, especially *will*, that are apt to arise when consciousness is stimulated, and lastly, consciousness itself.

But in thus passing criticism on this notable and interesting scheme of Groups (*khandhas*), this fact should be borne in mind.

It was one current division out of many others mentioned incidentally in the Pitakas, not to mention other Indian literature; it was also the most detailed, and was selected for a special purpose. This purpose was philosophical, rather than scientific.

Of other such divisions there was the ancient and convenient *nāma-rūpa*, literally, name and form, but actually meaning, for Buddhists, mind and body. Buddhists, in adopting *nāma-rūpa*, always explain it as meaning the contents of mind *plus* the material group. Then there was body and mind, or consciousness (*kāya* and *mano*, or *chitta*, or *viññana*); again body and feeling; body, feeling, consciousness, ideas; body, life, heat, consciousness; body *as* conscious, and "co-mental."

And, for the developing mental science of Buddhist culture, the cumbrous group scheme was dropped. Only the fourth and fifth groups were retained In them the fact and procedure of consciousness (and sub-consciousness) were investigated, and the contents of each phase or unit of consciousness were analyzed, including emotional and volitional factors. This evolution may be clearly seen in the mediæval standard handbook, translated as *Compendium of Philosophy*. But the transition is already begun in the Abhidhamma-Pitaka. In the first book,[1] consciousness is analyzed quite independently of

[1] See *Psychological Ethics*, pp. 1 ff., 26-29.

the group-scheme, and is then synthetized or summarized in terms of various categories, that of the *Khandha's* included, as one among others. The categories are then analyzed in turn, and under the fourth group (*sankhāra's*) we get a list of those concomitants which, in later method, were known chiefly as " mentals " or *chetas'ika's*.

For the exposition of Buddhist doctrine, religious and philosophical, the Five Groups lent themselves better than any current twofold division into body and mind. *Nāma-rūpa* was used in animistic and ātmanistic compositions. The soul-myths attaching all over the world to the significance of " a name " would not predispose Buddhism in its favour. But the opposing to the body, not one mental factor or two, but four, was apparently the result of a solicitude to omit no current term for mind that might serve as a rest and refuge for the insidious belief in Ātman or the eternal unchanging self. The way in which the Group-scheme is used in this connection is to set forth a fivefold delusion of supposing that any one of these five aggregates, either (1) is the soul, or (2) is an attribute of soul, or (3) is in the soul, or (4) contains the soul; just, for instance, (1) as flame and its colour may be considered one; or (2) as its shadow is an attribute of the tree; or (3) as the perfume is in the flower; or (4) as a casket contains a jewel.[1] Another

[1] *Sutta-Pit'aka, Patisambhidāmagga,* i. 143-5. Plotinus,

method is to show that if any one Group, taking these in turn, were the Self, it could (as God) dictate what and how it chose to be, body or mind. But since it is not free to choose, it cannot be that group.

This was at any rate the reason for the adoption of the fivefold division that commended itself to Buddhaghosa. Why, he asks, in his *Way of Purity,* did the Exalted One say there were five *Khandha's*, no less and no more? Because these not only sum up all classes of conditioned things, but they afford no foothold for soul and the animistic.

Finally, how did Buddhism conceive mind or mental aggregates, viewed as a phenomenal happening, and not as an underlying static substance?

Two impressive phenomena have aided Buddhism to state in general terms that which seemed fundamentally true about mind. These were sleep and flowing water. By the former, including the phenomenon of dreams, it pictured the *intermittent* nature of conscious mental life. By the latter, it placed in front the fact of the *continuity of an ever-changing identity.* Neither of these notions is explicitly developed by way of these similes in the Pāli Pitakas. Both notions are involved in the doctrines therein taught; and both underwent interesting

possibly from his Eastern travels, held with (3), viz., the body in the soul, as air is permeated by fire.—*Ennead* iv.

development. Let us first consider the older testimony.

In the following passage "mind," or conscious intelligent activity, is clearly taught as an intermittent phenomenon coming to pass *only* when suitable stimulation occurred. In the telling of it too, the style is vivid and pointed and emphatic, as though the teaching were more than usually urgent. Too long to give in full, the substance of the Sutta may be told in outline.

A bhikkhu or member of the Order, Sāti Fisher-son, gives out as the Master's teaching this heresy:[1] "It is mind (or consciousness or co-gnition, *vi-ññāna*) which persists and is reborn after death unchanged." The brethren protest, but he is firm. They report him, and the Master sends for him. "Is this true, Sāti?" "Yea, Lord, so do I understand you to teach." "What, Sāti, is that consciousness?" "That speaker and feeler, sir, who experiences the result of good and evil deeds done here or there." "Now, then, foolish man, from whom have you got such a doctrine as one of mine? Have I not taught you by many methods that consciousness arises from a cause: except from a cause there is no coming into being of consciousness?"

He then turns to the Bhikkhus, who testify to the truth of this. "And consciousness," he goes on, "is reckoned only in accordance

[1] *Majjhima-Nikāya.* "The Destruction of Craving" Sutta (38).

with the condition causing it; visual cognition from sight and seen object, idea from mind and mental object. Just as a fire is different according to its fuel."

"Do ye see that this has *become*, bhikkhus?

"Do ye see that the becoming is *according to the stimulus* (literally, the food)?

"Do ye see that if the stimulus cease, *then that which has become ceases*, bhikkhus?"

And so the catechism continues, enforcing the doctrine, the brethren responding duly.

This may suffice, as an example among others, to show that mind or consciousness was not only not to be regarded as the soul or *attā* under another name, but was not to be conceived as even a life-long immaterial substance. It was more after the nature of electrical energy, potential only till aroused by suitable stimuli.

There *was* a lifelong serial continuity, but it was not mind; it was the organic life. Considered subjectively this is subconsciousness. The Pāli word *bhavanga* expresses both (*a*) the objective aspect of vital functioning and (*b*) the subjective aspect of our sub-consciousness, or mental state, when we are not attending to anything, or that part of consciousness when we are attending to something not of that part. The term occurs in one book of the Abhidhamma-Pitaka, but it is only in the *Milinda* that we see the theory which was current. In that work (ii. 163), the functioning of the organism without consciousness, called *bhavanga-gati* (*gati* is " course," " going on "), is compared to dreamless sleep. A stimulus evoking consciousness had come, in Buddhaghosa's time, to be conceived as causing a vibration in the flow of the *bhavanga*. The reacting consciousness then arising was pictured as " cutting off " or damming the flow, which was resumed when attention (to some external or internal object) subsided. And in the *Compendium of Philosophy*—and probably centuries earlier—the river-simile appears: " So to those who have thus got rebirth, the same kind of consciousness (*chitta*), occupied with the same field of objects, starting straight away after the moment of rebirth, goes on, in the absence of any process of cognition, in unbroken flux, like the stream of a river, till the uprising of death-consciousness. And this flux, because it is a condition of being, is called continuance of the conditions of being." (*Compendium*, 152 f.)

" Like a river," comments a Burmese Buddhist of to-day, " which still maintains one constant form, one seeming identity, though not a single drop remains to-day of all the volume that composed that river yesterday." (*Op. cit.* Introd. Essay by S. Z. Aung, 9.)

So Herakleitus's fragment: " You cannot step twice into the same rivers, for fresh waters are ever flowing in upon you."

CHAPTER IV

THE NORM AS THE LAW OF CAUSATION

It was only possible in so short a compass to scratch the surface of the bold and remarkable position taken by Buddhism over against the theories of its day. We must perforce get on, nor try to deal with the subject in the light of the criticism it evoked in its native land. As we go, we may learn more of the ground so far traversed. For the central tenets are so closely interrelated, that to consider any one throws light on the rest.

Let us then turn to the second implication of the term Dhamma. "*Dhammo ti hetu,*" wrote Buddhaghosa: "*dhamma means condition,*" or *cause*. And, to go centuries back and repeat the Pitaka phrase :—" Investigation of Dhamma=insight into cause." Now in this connection I find a salient feature in Buddhist philosophy, namely: In place of theories on this or that agency as constituting the Source, the informing, sustaining Principle, and the End of this present order called world or universe, Buddhists concentrated their attention on the order of things itself. This order they conceived as a multitudinous and continual coming-to-be and passing-away in everything. And this constant transition, change, or becoming was not capricious, nor ordained for the occasion, nor pre-ordained, but went on by way of natural causation. This conclusion I have now to justify.

We have seen that, with regard to the general belief in an in-dwelling, or circumambient, or pervading soul or spirit or ego, permanent, unchanging, unsuffering, Buddhism took the standpoint, two thousand four hundred years ago, of our own Hume of two centuries ago. It would have welcomed his saying—modern Buddhists who have studied our philosophy do welcome it—that in seeking for the self he always "tumbled on some particular perception." They have ever judged that when we so seek, we find, not agent, but just process; a changing bundle of functions, but no unchanging functioner nor spectator behind it all. The Vedântist doctrine of the Upanishads said: "Let none try to find out what speech is, let him know the speaker; let none try to find out what visible object, action, mind is, let him know the seer, the agent, the thinker."[1] In Buddhaghosa we read the categorical opposite "Anything whatever within called soul (*attā*) who sees, who moves the limbs, etc., there is not."[2]

Now note the way in which, centuries

[1] *Kaushītakī Up.*, iii. 8.

[2] *Sumangala-Vilāsinī*, i. 195

earlier than Buddhaghosa, the absolutist position had been corrected in the Pitakas :—"It is no fit question to ask : Who experiences contact? Who is it that feels? *This* is the right way to question : *Conditioned by what*, is there contact? *Conditioned by what*, is there feeling?"[1] Here is the statement which Buddhists might choose to place beside Hume's "tumbling on his particular perceptions" instead of on to a general essence. When we seek, they might say, we find only a conditioned happening; not a perduring entity, nor a mere fortuitous succession, but something happening in consequence of something that had gone before.

In their mental science of Abhidhamma, they call this order of conditioned happening or process, by the term *vīthi*, road, course or process. In more popular exposition, as in the *Milinda*, they figure the idea under various similes, as thus :—

"King Milinda : 'Does perception arise wherever sensation of sight arises?' 'Yes, sire.' 'Which arises first?' 'First sight, then perception.' 'Then does sight issue as it were a command to perception : spring up there after me? or does thought command sight : I will spring up where you do?' 'No, sire, there is no such intercourse.' 'Then how is it, that perception arises when sight arises?' 'Because of there being a sloping down, a door, a habit, an association.' 'How is

[1] *Samyutta-Nikāya*, ii. 13.

that ? ' 'Well, sire, when it rains, where will the water go ? ' 'It will follow the slope of the ground.' 'And if it were to rain again ? ' 'The water would go the same way as the former water.' 'What then ? Does the former water issue a command to the latter water. . . . ? ' 'No, there is no intercourse between the two. Each goes its way because of the slope of the ground.' 'Just so, sire, is it in sensation and perception. . . . All that happens, happens through *natural slope.*' "

The door-metaphor (*dvāra*, like John Bunyan's Eye-gate, Ear-gate, etc.), as the habitual means of exit by a certain road in a city, is together with road or street (*vīthi*) the standard psychological metaphor for avenue of sense. Again, the carts of the merchandise caravans would go out by a *habitual* order of going. And the arts of arithmetic and writing, difficult at first, become easy through *association* set up by practice.[1] That everything we can know by way of the avenues of sense, including the Dhamma itself, was something that had become (*bhūta*), was conditioned (*sankhătă*), had arisen-because-of (*paticcha-samuppanna*), lay at the heart of that Dhamma. " He who discerns origin by way of cause, he discerns the Dhamma ; he who discerns the Dhamma he discerns origin by way of cause." [2]

[1] *Questions of King Milinda,* i. 89 ff.

[2] *Majjhima-Nikāya,* i. 191 ; *Dīgha,* iii. 275.

It may be objected here that the three terms are redundant, conditioned being synonymous with caused. It is true that, at least in Burmese Abhidhamma, they now mean the same idea. *Sankhata* is literally made, put together, compound. But Mr. S. Z. Aung writes: "Of course what is compound is always caused. But it is the idea of causation that is chiefly implied." (*Compendium*, 273.) If, however, we consult a passage in the Sutta Pitaka, we find three essential or necessary "marks"—our logic would say "properties"—of anything that is *sankhata*; "genesis is revealed, passing away is revealed, and the dividing-line of the static (moment) is revealed; these three are the marks of the *sankhata*."[1] Hence, in the notion originally expressed by this term, we get, not exactly what we now understand, in philosophy, by "conditioned,"—"that which is pre-requisite in order that something may be,"—but rather that which is supplied by our word "organic."

Hereby we see how interwoven are those three concepts; become, *sankhata*, and caused. And they were held in such a way as to elude the metaphysical problems of (*a*) realism and idealism, and of (*b*) mechanism and atomism.

(*a*) Theories akin to the "Only being is; non-being is not; there is no becoming" of Parmenides (b. about 515 B.C.), and its opposite seem to have been prevalent in North India perhaps half a century *before* the Greek

[1] *Aṅguttara-Nikāya*, i. 152.

philosopher wrote his poem on "the way of truth and the way of opinion," in which he declared his Absolutist philosophy. This is anyway the comment which, in the Sutta-Pitaka, is said to have been made on two occasions by the Buddha:[1] "The world for the most part, Kacchāna, holds either to a belief in being, or to a belief in non-being. But for one who by right insight sees as it really is how the world comes to pass, there is no non-being in the world. And for one who by right insight sees as it really is how the world passes away, there is no being (literally: beingness: *atthitā*) in the world. Everything *is*: this, Kacchāna, is one extreme view. Everything *is not*: this is the second extreme view. Avoiding both these extremes, the Buddha teaches the Norm by the Mean" (middle). And the gist of this Doctrine of the Mean is that life, as we know it, is a becoming, or coming to be, through one state of the organism, mental and bodily, inducing a "related" state, as consequent to antecedent.

Whether Parmenides derived his opinions perhaps through his Pythagorean teachers, from Indian ideas or not, we do not know. Nor, in the absence of any fuller statement of the former extreme, alluded to by the Buddha, can we say, whether that view coincided with the position taken by Parmenides. But some coincidence seems probable. That which really is, said Parmenides,

[1] *Samyutta-Nikāya*, ii. 17; iii. 135.

behind all the fleeting shows of sense, is ever and eternally present. If it were past and gone, or not yet, you could not think of it, for you cannot think of what does not exist. It cannot have become; "what need could have made it arise later rather than sooner? Therefore must it either be altogether, or be not at all."

That which we remember therefore, or anticipate is, according to him, not the phenomena that are passed away, or yet to come, but the ever-present really existent.

The parallels between the thought of Parmenides and of Plato, who thought on his lines, on the one hand, and Indian Absolutist or Ātmanistic philosophy on the other, are frequently pointed out in Professor Deussen's *History of Philosophy*. There is for instance a good parallel to the sentence quoted above, where it is denied that the Real can come to be. But it occurs in a work that is centuries later than either Parmenides, or the views referred to by the Buddha, although it was probably directed against the doctrine of the then declining Buddhism of North India. Thus in one verse of this work we read:—
"Being cannot become, for then it were only illusion. Who lets anything come to be, lets that come to be that was already there."[1]

We see here (1) that the Buddhist standpoint;—that instead of considering things or souls as eternal, fixed entities, beings, or forms

[1] *Māndukya-Kārikā.*

we should think of them as coming to be from other things that had become,—offered a way out of the older deadlock, and was probably fresh at the time, and place; (2) that later hostile philosophy met this standpoint and rejected it, just as, in Greece, Parmenides met and rejected the "All things are in flux" of Herakleitus.

(*b*) There appears to have been, parallel with these Absolutist beliefs, a good deal of scepticism current when Buddhism arose. Such theories were probably a more extreme recoil from the former than anything put forward by Buddhism. They amounted to this; that once we surrender, from the heaven our forefathers believed in, and the earth we see, all transcendental realities, all first cause, all personal intelligent driving principle, nothing remains but "a fortuitous concourse of atoms," or at best the blind unintelligent working of a machine come no one knows how into operation, drifting no man knows whither. The most important of these sceptic schools was that of the Ājī'vakas, whose leader, Makkhăli Gosāla, is thus said to have formulated his position:—"Beings become depraved without cause or conditions; they become morally pure also without cause. Our attainments do not depend on effort or action, either of our own or of others. There is no human energy or power that is effective. All things that have life, creatures, and souls, are without inherent force. They are bent this way and that by the necessity of their specific nature."

Another sophistical school, headed by Aj'ĭtă of the Hair-garment, taught that there was no fruit nor result of good or evil deeds; no other world, nor was this one real; nor had parents nor any former lives any efficacy with respect to this life. Saintly thinkers could see no farther into the truth of things than others. And nothing that we can do prevents all of us alike being wholly brought to an end at death.

These pessimistic and nihilistic views the Buddhists classed together as typically "wrong (*micchā*) opinions," and they opposed to them a categorical contradiction in a positive formula, constituting "right (*sammā*) opinion." The Buddha, moreover, expressly took the stand of a teacher of effective action, or *kammavādin*, and that repeatedly, in open opposition, and in forcible terms:—

"Just as, bhikkhus, of all kinds of woven robes, a hair-garment is known to be the least desirable" (is there here a side-allusion to Aj'ĭtă? Buddhaghosa passes it over); "cold in cold weather, hot in the heat, unpleasant to the touch, so of all the many assertions by recluses, the Makkhali theory is the most undesirable. He, foolish man, believes and declares there is no effective action (going on), no effected action (the result of effective action), no indwelling energy. Herein he rejects that which all past Buddhas have declared, all future Buddhas will declare, and which I now, the Buddha, declare. I, even I, declare that there is effective action, resultant action, indwelling energy."[1]

Now in accepting what, on the surface, is the common-sense view, that actions have results, and that what happens, happens because of something, the Buddhists know well enough that just to acquiesce in that view was not enough for reasoned knowledge, or philosophy. They knew also very well, that the sceptics were not flouting merely the man in the street. Neither Makkhali nor Aj'ĭtă would have denied that if you pushed him, he might fall down. But they might be prepared to deny, first, that any original creative energy arose in you, next that anything called energy or force passed from you as cause on to them, effecting the fall. Some demon, or chance agency perhaps worked, *then* you had an impulse, then somehow your arm went out (not your mind), then Makkhali went over. And all this you put together and said: "See the efficient cause and its effect!" All pure hypothesis on your part, to explain a little that you saw, and much that you did not see, by a pretty but fanciful theory. What *is* cause?

The Buddhists' reply, in its older form and on the surface, is more logical and scientific than metaphysical. It runs very well on all fours with our own modern logic and our

[1] *Anguttara-Nikāya*, i. 286.

physical science. And we ourselves practically admit that we can get no working metaphysical definition of cause and effect. To say that when A causes B, an influence, force, action, or what not, X, passes from A to B is not reckoned very convincing metaphysic. We long staved off the difficulty with the convenient Aristotelian phrase "efficient cause," or that which makes the effect to be what it is. But since Thomas Brown and J. Stuart Mill, we in this country at least have let it suffice to say, that "we have no idea of anything in the way of efficiency beyond *regularity of sequence*," and to leave the matter with the text-books on logic:—"The cause of an event means the circumstances which must have preceded in order that the event should happen," or again: "That every event is the result or sequel of some previous event, or events, without which it could not have happened, and which, being present, it must take place."[1]

So far for ourselves. The ancient Buddhist formula presents a parallel view. Leaving speculations as to beginning and end, it says, all *dhamma's*, all things-as-known, happen from causes. And a cause was that or those things, the presence of which was necessary for a certain succeeding thing or things known as result. And so centrally important was this uniformity in sequence reckoned that it is

[1] Jevons's *Lessons in Logic*, and *Dictionary of Philosophy and Psychology*.

called "the Dhamma." "Put aside," the Buddha is represented as saying to a speculative Jain, "put aside these questions of the beginning and the hereafter. I will teach you the Dhamma:—'that being present, this becomes; from the arising of that, this arises. That being absent, this does not become; from the cessation of that, this ceases'" (*Majjhima-N.*, Sutta 79).

Surely a notable milestone in the history of human ideas that a man reckoned for ages by thousands as the Light not of Asia only but of the World, and the saviour from sin and misery, should call this little formula his Norm or Gospel, or at least one aspect of that Gospel! There can be no question as to its being an interesting link between ancient Buddhism and our own thought, whatever else we may conclude about it. So interesting indeed is it, so supreme did this universal causality rank in the Buddhist doctrine as a point of view, and a sound method; so much have we tended to overlook method and point of view, and lay emphasis only on the matters *to which the method was applied*, that it will be well to consider the subject more at length.

In calling the Buddhist emphasis on the causal order of the world a point of view and a method, we use their own terms. Sometimes they call the quest of an earnest inquirer into the truth of things as a seeking after Good, Method or System (*ñyāya*), and Dhamma.

Thus the Buddha, among the last Words ascribed to him, said :—

> But twenty-nine was I when I renounced
> The world, Subhadda, seeking after Good,
> For fifty years and yet another year
> Since I went out, a pilgrim have I been,
> Through the wide realm of System and of Law—
> Outside thereof no victory can be won.[1]

And elsewhere, in sweeping away, for religion and ethics, all barriers of class or caste, ethical progress is summed up as a striving on a basis of morality after Good, System, and Dhamma. Now system, method (*ñyāya*), is defined as follows :—" And what, house-father, is this Ariyan method which one who is fit to attain the highest has by insight well seen and well penetrated ? "

" This : that the Ariyan disciple well and thoroughly attends to the arising-by-way-of-cause, namely :—That being present, this becomes ; because that arises, this arises, etc."[2]

Hereupon follows the standard and staple *illustration and application* of the logical, or philosophical formula : Namely,

Past Lives. { because of ignorance, actions,
" actions, (fresh) consciousness (causing rebirth),

[1] *Dialogues*, ii, 167.
[2] *Samyutta-Nikāya*, v. 388.

Present Span of Life.	because of that	consciousness, (new) mind and body,
	,,	mind and body, sense organs,
	,,	sense-organs, contact,
	,,	contact, feeling,
	,,	feeling, craving,
	,,	craving, grasping,
	,,	grasping (the disposition for) becoming (or rebirth)
Future Lives.	,,	becoming, rebirth,
	,,	rebirth, decay, death, grief, mourning, pain, sorrow and despair.

"Such is the coming to pass of this entire mass of ill."

I have given this famous "Chain or Wheel of the Twelve Bases" with the explanatory terms supplied by the Commentators. Buddhists from the first have recognized it as "deep":—"deep is this doctrine of events as arising from causes, and it looks deep too!"—but they have not admitted it to be incomprehensible, as have some European critics. The chief difficulty has never existed for them, namely, that of regarding the twelve as all applying to one individual life. For Buddhists "life" is an infinite matter, at least, a matter without finite *beginning*. Hence it contains within itself an infinite number of what we call individual lives, or spans of life. And it is as simple a matter for them to divide up the formula into past, present and future spans of life, or rebirths, as for us to sketch parents, self, and descendants in a genealogical scheme. Buddhaghosa accordingly explains the scheme without hesitation as involving more than one such span.

The fact that life as we know it is largely made up of painful and sorrowful experiences is the foundation from which Buddhism as religion, ethics, philosophy, takes its start. It claims as the supreme merit in the Dhamma, that it has recognized this fact, understood it causally, and surmounted its effects.

But the prominence given in the doctrine to this fact of Ill, or the ills of life, and the accounting for those ills, in the foregoing formula, by a string of natural causes, have proved for students of the doctrine the supreme, nay, the only interesting features in it. The emphasis on the general method or point of view, as illustrated by this stock genealogy of Ill, is relatively passed over.

Now a comparative study of the many contexts of the formula, in the Pitakas, may show that the general principle involved, namely, natural causation, was at least as important as the classic illustration and application of the principle.

For instance, it will be admitted that, if the Wheel, when quoted, is adduced solely in order to teach "the uprising of this entire mass of Ill," or of any link therein, the discourse, in which it occurs, would have the same object, solely or in part. But in ninety-six Suttas, in which the Wheel occurs, only one-sixth are directly concerned with the fact and causes of pain and sorrow. The "great discourse" on bases,[1] in which the Wheel is discussed at length, is not directly so concerned. Of the remaining Suttas, sixteen are so many statements upholding the truth of the evolution of phenomena by way of natural causation. Then there are seven which discuss rebirth, and eight, the destruction of craving. Here, it is true, we get discussion on Segments in the Wheel, but not on Ill as such. Another is the discourse rebuking Sāti's heresy, dealt with in the last chapter. The lessons there inculcated are not on hedonistic, *i.e.*, concerned with feeling, nor moral. They have nothing to emphasize as to Pain. They are concerned to repudiate the substitution of *mind* for *soul*, and they affirm that mind is a contingent phenomenon, *happening* by way of cause and effect. Four Suttas are interesting to our inquiry herein, that *loka*, or the world of sense-perception, is *substituted* in the Wheel for Ill, serving, it was felt, also as an application of the method. Lastly, thirty-six Suttas emphasize the importance of mastering the principle of "Causal genesis."

Thus we get over one-third pointing to the principle, and only about one-sixth pointing to the subject illustrated.

[1] *Dialogues* ii. 50 ff. "Wheel" is a later term.

Again, the order of sequence in the Segments of the Wheel is not the main tenet. Had this been so, that order would always be the same. But now and then it is varied. So also is the number of the Segments. The first two are sometimes omitted; so are the first five. One presentation gives nos. 3, 4, 2, 11, 12 only, and in this order. And in one Sutta the antecedents of Ill are given as "desire, attachment, indulgence, lusting-after." Now in this discourse, the subject is expressly "suffering": the difficulty of enduring persecutions with energy, mindfulness and serenity. And the brethren are encouraged to consider that they are well advanced—"have wrought much"—if they, remembering the conditioned nature of the five factors of the organism, note that such and such is the way in which they are grouped and combined and co-ordinated, all coming to pass by way of cause—had not the Exalted One said that caused-origin was Dhamma, and conversely?—and that just as they knew the causes of Ill, so by removing the causes, could they make the effect to cease.[1] Here, had the chief import of the Wheel been instruction in the genesis of pain and sorrow, we should certainly have had it given in full. But it is entirely absent. Only the standpoint as to causation is associated with it.

For all that, the fact of Ill and its causes holds in nearly every case the last word in

[1] The apostle Sāriputta is speaking. *Majjh. Nik.* i. 191.

this curious old rune. And the records tell how the fact and the sequence of those causes dawned ever on the mind of a Buddha, as he wrestled for light on the problems of the menace and mystery of life. We need then, in considering the importance of the Wheel in the Dhamma, always to keep in view this dual aspect of it. Namely, that it is a way of explaining phenomena, and again, that the most impressive world-phenomenon to be explained is that of suffering. The latter standpoint is that of man as receptive or perceptive—he *feels*;—the former is that of man intellective or interpreting—he *thinks*.

How far the rune was entirely a Buddhist creation we shall never know. It is by no means the only teaching so expressed, *i.e.*, by way of cause—effect }—effect, in Indian
cause }
lore. In the old aphorisms of the philosophic school called Sānkhya, there is a similar but fragmentary formula, giving the genesis of mental factors: "From nature, intellect, thence self-apperception, thence the sixteen-fold set; from five thereof the five elements." And it has been claimed that Buddhism, drawing from this school, expanded its formula from the above. This is not a highly plausible theory. The Sānkhya was not Ātmanistic; nevertheless, as an Absolutist metaphysic it would have been repugnant to Buddhism, had the latter found it current.

There may, however, have been some older

rune bearing on the facts of life and mind, from which both schools borrowed. The näive mould in which the belief is cast is no doubt primitive enough. We think of our nursery rhyme: "The cat began to kill the rat, the rat began to gnaw the rope," and so on . . till, corresponding to the conclusion as to Ill, we end: "And so the old woman got home that night." This, we learn from folk-lorists, is one of the most wide-spread of prehistoric folk-runes of the class called "accumulative jingles." It is more to be wondered at, that so few ancient doctrines adopted as mnemonics its simple, impressive sequences, than that two systems made use of it. Neither body of doctrine was at all likely to cultivate the form of the rune as effective in and through its jingling cadence. There is a good deal of such abracadabra in the Indian literature that has grown up around altar and priestly chant, but Buddhism and Sānkhya have no such traditions.

Hence, neither its antiquity, nor the accident of its form, nor even its separate links, all of which are taught severally, more or less, in the Pitakas, can account for the high value attached to the formula of causal genesis. But in its affirmation of a natural order, put forward for the first time as a gospel for all, in antithesis to the animism about them: here truly is an impressive iconoclasm and a bold stand, costing an effort we can scarce realize. *Too* great a forward stride to take and maintain in India. Not too great for the maintenance of Dhamma in the South Asian centres, remote from skilled Absolutist dialectic. Still in Burma and Ceylon is taught the Law of Happening by way of cause, thus formulated some eight hundred years ago: "This law is a mode marked by the simple condition of a phenomenon happening, when its sole invariable antecedent phenomenon happens." Then follows the Wheel, and an analysis of it.[1]

But it is one thing to teach this as textbook logic to blithe, acquiescent youths in the monastery schools, another to have first discerned all that it involved, when brought in to solve the riddles of birth, decay and death. *The fact* of suffering does not come as a revelation to the Buddha, thinking hard beneath his Bodhi-tree, nor the fairly obvious causes of it. That fact drove him restless from home, station and ease. It was the process of the natural, necessary, universal law, by which all things, bodily and mental, *happened*, or became nascent, static, and expiring. Pain and suffering are not the thought that seizes him, but:—

"Coming to pass! Coming to pass! At that thought there arose in me a Vision into things not called before to mind. And knowledge arose, insight arose, wisdom arose, light arose. . . . Passing away! Passing away! At that thought there arose in

[1] *Compendium of Philosophy*, p. 187.

me a vision into things not called before to mind. . . ." Not uncaused and casually, nor by the fiat of Īsh'vara—Lord—whether Indra, Soma, Varu*n*a, Brahmā—did events happen, painful or otherwise; not, it seemed to him, was it true, literally or poetically conceived, to hold that ruling deities, angry every day at man's shortcomings, distributed sorrows in their anger.[1] Events came impelled by preceding conditions, causes that man could by intelligence and goodwill study and govern, suspend or intensify.

Do I seem to be reading contents that are not Indian, not early Indian, into these old records? At all events, the very early commentarial tradition from which Buddhaghosa drew his materials saw and realized such implications in the doctrine of the Wheel. In explaining the name for it: "Happening-by-way-of-cause," he points out[2] that it excludes all theories of absolutism, nihilism, chance, irregular causation and indeterminism. . . The wheel of Becoming is without known beginning, lacking both maker . . . such as Brahmā . . . and percipient "I." "For each consequent proceeds by reason of its antecedent." As usual it is the first two theories that, as the most prevalent, call for his special attention. Namely, that there

[1] Job xxi. 17.

[2] *Way of Purity*, ch. xvii. This is now in process of being edited and translated by Professor Lanman and Pundit Kosambi.

is no persistent ego reaping results in one life, which It has sown in a previous life, although, again, it is no alien ego who reaps, but one who is the resultant, the creature, the evolved successor and representative of the former.

Into this, which we may call the Buddhist theory of efficient, or passed-on cause, we can better enter presently. But in so far as the very definite comment cited above expands faithfully the earlier text, the doctrine compressed into the Wheel implied as decided a negation of any absolute cause as did the doctrine of Demokritus and Leukippus: namely that nothing happens save through a cause and of necessity—a doctrine which the latter published perhaps half a century after the Buddha's death.

Willingly or unwillingly, humanity has let die the writings of both the Greek fathers of modern science. Had not the current of philosophical thought been resumed in, and steered by two thinkers of such genius as Plato and Aristotle—the one pure Absolutist, the other modified Absolutist—the whole philosophy of the West might conceivably have flowed along a channel in which it would earlier have approached the informing principle of the Buddhist doctrine of cause. As it came to pass, Europe learned from those two latter thinkers compromise and comprehensiveness, learned, in other words, to believe in a universe governed partly by necessity and partly by chance, learned to combine belief in unchanging natural law with belief in first and final causes.

So gradually has the realm of regular, causal sequence encroached upon that of the casual and the arbitrary, that we can trace, in the early history of European thought, no such milestone marking where the notion of a universe, governed as to its every movement and happening, was brought home to the minds of men—to the mind of one man. With us philosophy and religion have never blended, and science has expanded independently of both. Hence we see no such intellectual earthquake in the history of our ideas as was caused half a century ago by that extension of the law of causation: the theory of evolution. Most of my readers will have no personal memory of the time. But we have only to read the letters and biographies of contemporaries to see what searchings of heart, yea, what a sword that theory brought among us.

It soon appeared, however, that even evolution fitted, as well as natural causation generally, into the traditional compromise and comprehensiveness of our standpoints. So that, with our science and our philosophy and our religion marching along side by side in an armed truce, and a judicious amount of liberty of speech conceded to each, intellectual earthquakes throughout educated circles are improbable events. The full significance of natural causation still comes to birth, but it is in the mind of this or that thoughtful youth and maiden. I can remember some such "vision" borne in on my own experience when, in a text-book on brain and mind, I realized that the procedure of mental and of cerebral phenomena also went on by the Dhamma of cause and effect.

But how had it been with us, if in olden time some prophet had arisen, who had seen, in a vision of universal natural law, not a philosophic theory only, nor a scientific induction, but a saving Truth, a Religion, whereby he might purify both his own beliefs and redeem mankind from error and delusion? We could not then say the history of our thought presented no milestone recording the outcrop of such a notion. Possibly there was some such epoch-marking day, when Demokritus produced his *Diakosmos*, now lost, but on account of which he was hailed in the Levant as a great prophet and teacher of mankind.

In the history of Indian thought, on the other hand, we can point to such a day, and such a milestone; we can discern the significance of the law of universal natural causation breaking in on a great mind, racked by doubts and difficulties, with a flash of intuition. The law reveals itself as an actual, present and eternal order. And he, the Tathā'gata, the Man-who-had-thus-come, was there to penetrate and master it, and to deliver it as a

Norm, as a true standard of views and values, to the world.[1]

No such crisis of thought is patent in the sacerdotal, or mystical, or philosophical literature of the Brahmin culture, even though that literature is practically co-extensive with Indian religion and philosophy. The Upanishads are widest and most original in their scope; but those ranked as oldest show a naïve animism, those held to be later reveal a much more advanced maturity of thought. We may, for instance, contrast such a passage as: The Ātman deliberated: I will send forth worlds; he then formed the person . . . he brooded over him, and . . . a mouth burst forth like an egg . . . with this: "Should time, or nature, or necessity, or chance, or the elements, or the person (soul) be considered as the *cause*?"[2] And there is nothing between these two stages of mental output to show any transitional expansion, accompanied by an intellectual crisis. In fact, as in other matters, the idea is at the back of our minds, as we read and compare, that Buddhism itself had been the intrusive influence, fermenting in circles outside its own radius.

In the seventy-two stanzas of the Sānkhya-Kārikā again, 25 per cent. contain some

[1] *Samyutta N.* ii. 25.

[2] *Aitareyya* and *Shvetāsvatara* Upanishads, reckoned as one of the four oldest, and as eleventh among the twelve oldest, respectively, by Regnaud.

consciously generalized affirmation about cause and effect. We see that the notion of cause in the abstract is quite a mature and polished instrument of thought. No less in the Yoga-Sūtra too, the origin of which is also lost in the obscurity of the past, do we find allusions to causality wielded as an abstract idea. The earliest literature of the Jains is nearly totally inaccessible to us, and awaits its editor, let alone translator. We only know that in its mediæval books is an atomistic theory not without interest.

So far then it is only in the Pāli-Pitakas that we come up against the actual effort of the mind to get at a more scientific view of world-order. And that effort is marked with the freshness and vigour of a new advance in intellectual expansion. The importance and the gravity of the conviction is affirmed with the utmost emphasis, both in the Pitakas and in the orthodox literature of the fifth century.

But, it is said, Buddhism was a gospel promulgated by laymen, chiefly by sons of nobles and burgesses, and preached to all sorts and conditions of men. Such teachers would naturally regard as new and wonderful truths, notions and axioms which had long been familiar to the more esoteric, philosophical schools of the day, and which were truisms in dialectical metaphysic.

This may very likely be true for the first decades of the Buddhist movement. It expressly professed to be a missionary and democratic movement. Its founder was driven to leave the world to gain his own soul—to use an un-Buddhistic quotation. But he decided, with sore misgiving, to quit the mental peace and repose he had won in solitude, to go back among men, and to seek after those who had ears to hear, or as the Buddhist record says, had eyes to see. He left the shady tree for the crossways, or, as we say, the study-armchair for the market-place. When the doctrine so grew as to cover the land with colleges and settlements, and to be the most highly favoured cult of the country, it would naturally and inevitably annex the best thought and learning in the country, as was the case for a thousand years with the Christian Church.

But the human mind may acquire a general notion, and yet so confine the range thereof by definition and axiom, that it remains sterile, and all the great world-moving induction latent in it may lie unheeded. It is the mind or minds who expand a concept for us under some Bo-tree—make wide the implications of thought, and tell us what they see—these it is who create the wisdom that is fruitful among men, theirs is the utterance that is the true evolutionary cry of travail and new birth.

Such a birth-cry comes to us from these old Pitakas, the cry of humanity, as it were, beholding " a vision into things not called before to mind." And these are the supreme movements of life. "The day of days, the great day of the feast of life, is that in which the inward eye opens to the unity in things, to the omnipresence of law. If truth come to our minds, we suddenly expand to its dimensions, as if we grew to worlds. We are as law-givers; we speak for nature; we prophesy and divine."[1] And in the history of philosophy, whether we are listening to the truly originating seer, or to minds reacting to his influence, nothing is more illuminating for our efforts to interpret that history, than to catch the intelligence in the act of ascending to a fresh vantage-point in its interpretation of the world. We note and hail it, as the Buddhist legend hailed its founder's advent as teacher:—

> As on a crag, on crest of mountain standing,
> A man might watch the people far below,
> E'en so do thou, O Wisdom fair, ascending,
> O Seer of all, the terraced heights of Truth,
> Look down, from grief released, upon the nations
> Sunken in grief, oppressed with birth and age;
> Arise, thou Hero! Conqueror in the battle!
> Thou freed from debt! Lord of the pilgrim band!
> Walk the world o'er, sublime and blessed Teacher,
> Teach us the Truth; there are who'll understand.

And until research among documents that survive, or delving in sands for such as have been lost, brings to us other testimony to some such vision of universal law revealed as a

[1] Emerson.

message of vital import to the world, a unique interest must attach to the Pāli Pitakas, for presenting to us this evolutionary moment —an interest not only for the history of Indian thought, but for the history of human ideas in general.

CHAPTER V

THE NORM AS MORAL LAW

We may now proceed to the third stated implication in that pregnant term Dhamma, and connect it with the foregoing considerations. This is what we should call a moral or ethical import:—

> **"Not of a like result are right and wrong"**
> (*dhamma, adhamma*).

We are not concerned just here to consider in detail the moral or ethical code of Buddhism. It has now and again been put forward that Buddhism is neither religion nor philosophy, but only a system of morals or ethics, in so far as it contains anything beyond mere negations. It would not be well to meet this assertion with the hasty generalization, that such a system could never have, at any time, commanded attention, respect and adherence among all classes in India, as was the case with Buddhism. We are scarcely in a position as yet to dogmatize about the essentials in successful gospels. India is wide enough and old enough to have found place and time for systems acceptable to all classes of mind and temperament, and for conjunctures favourable to possibly more propaganda than we deem likely to succeed. Asoka's edicts carved on rock and pillar are, for the most part, injunctions to his subjects to act "according to Dhamma." And that seems, in these imperial messages to the man in the street, to be tantamount to acting wisely, honourably, kindly. "The Dhamma is good," says one edict, "but what is the Dhamma? The having but little, in one's mind, of the intoxicants (sensuality, lust for life, mere opinion, ignorance); doing many benefits to others; compassion, liberality, truth, purity." There are 34 of these edicts surviving, distributed over practically the whole of India, and it is noteworthy that only in one of them is allusion made to the word of the Buddha as such. The only *sanction*, definitely invoked as a motive force, is the welfare of the individual, now and hereafter, resulting from his acting according to Dhamma, together with the welfare of beings in general.

The edicts quote some of the Suttas in the Pāli Pitakas by name:—what then is the position taken in those scriptures with respect to this sanction of well-doing? Do they teach any fundamental principle why M or N should be habitually and systematically good? For it is not likely that a doctrine, so virile in its appeal to the intellect, in its confidence in the power of intelligence, as is Buddhism, should be content to say, as if to children, or to persons in subjection: "Do this! Be that! Never mind why!" Even if we do not find a ground of morals explicitly stated, shall we not read one between the lines? Does not every code of morals for free men and women imply a ground, or reason of action? "There is always," wrote Robert Louis Stevenson, "a ruling spirit behind the code of rules, an attitude, a relation, a point of the compass, in virtue of which we conform, or dissent." "And thus," that gracious voice goes on, "to learn aright from any teacher, we must first of all, like a historical artist, think ourselves into sympathy with his position. . . . Briefly, if a saying is hard to understand, it is *because we are thinking of something else.*"[1]

What then is the Buddhist position as to why people should be good? We are not here discussing that higher ethical level of what India called the freed mind: the character that had got past troubling itself about results. We are just now on the level of character which asks: What shall I gain, what will happen to me, if I am good, if I am wicked? Buddhism as a national creed must have met, must yet meet this sort of inquiry, as well as that of less practical aspiration.

[1] *Lay Morals.* The opening pages of Mr. Fielding's *Soul of a People* contain a pathetic confession of an inquirer baffled by thinking all the while of "something else."

It nas not been easy for Western thought to get at it, just because that thought is so often thinking of something else. It tends to judge, at its first contact with Buddhist doctrine, that there is no gain or retribution worth speaking of. We have in mind what certain words mean for us according to our notions fitted into them—notions derived from our traditional way of looking at things. I have experienced this sort of difficulty to no small extent in inquiring into the fundamental principles of Buddhism. And I seldom meet with a European work on Buddhism in which I do not see the same sort of inquiry hampered by the same sort of hindrance. It may help us to look out for these "something elses" of our traditional standpoints as we go on, and to endeavour, by Stevenson's suggestion, to become historical artists, thinking ourselves into intellectual sympathy with the Buddhist position.

When we say "nature," "natural law," we do not usually include in it any "moral law." We include under it the certain sequence of a green shoot grown from seed sown in a suitable soil and climate. But we do not, with equal certainty, affirm a sequent measure of happiness to the doer of a good deed, or of unhappiness to the doer of a bad deed. We do affirm this with respect to good and bad actions taken in the lump, and in the long run. But we admit that many good deeds are in this life unrewarded, that much wrong-doing and crime goes undetected, many a wicked person dying in comfort and prosperity. Those who look for compensation and retribution hereafter rely on the fiat of a divine judge. Those who hold that no good act is lost rely on the omniscient care of a divine providence. *Why* we should do good, is for some a divinely implanted intuition, guided by a divinely implanted conscience; for some a conclusion based on human experience of the benign results of good action in general.

Let us now look at the Buddhist point of view. Buddhists concentrated their attention not on a cause or mover of the order of things physical and moral, but on the order itself. They held that this order was one of constant universal change, organically conceived, *i.e.*, as growth and decay, and conceived as proceeding by cause and effect. Things become, as the sequels of certain assignable other things having become.

That may all be true, we say, and intellectually noteworthy, but it leaves us cold and morally indifferent. The Buddhists may have seen, in what has seemed to many the mere mechanism of a soulless universe, an eternal orderly procedure, but we do not see how they could draw thence any motive making for righteousness, let alone piety and devotion. Ātmanism, from one point of view, may have been a kind of elephantiasis of the Ego. From another, it suffused the human being with a splendour of divinity, beside and in which all that was mean and vile shrivelled and died. What is there then, or was there originally in Buddhism, to move people to seek good and avoid evil? Was it not to a conjuncture of circumstances that it owed its first moral enthusiasm? And does it owe now no moral force to its mixture with animistic systems?

Such considerations could not be shelved in any complete account of the growth of Buddhism. For such an account would have to render intelligible why it was that a movement which started as the backward swing of the religious and philosophical pendulum away from Ātmanism, ritualism and formalism, should not have remained as the Protestant and negating attitude of a few reformers. It would have to account for its expansion into a manifold and remarkable body of culture in India, and for its survival as a venerable and remarkably loyal tradition of religious philosophy in the Theravādin centres of the present day, not to mention the many Mahāyānist schools in the far East. It would have to enable us to realize the positive and drawing power of early Buddhism attracting thousands to itself, in India and in its mission fields, in the centuries of its expansion. It would have to show some plausible reason why that which so many critics among us call gloomy, pessimistic, arid, wooden, irrational, still sits enthroned in lands where pessimism, asceticism, decadence and vice are not more present, are even less in evidence, than in lands not professedly Buddhist, and where the national temperament that abides loyal to the ancient Dhamma is, for the most part, sunny and cheerfully, if not deeply, pious. Any explanation of its wide diffusion and long-lived tenacity must demonstrate wherein it could commend itself, at first and subsequently, to the intelligence of the thoughtful, as well as to the hearts of the million.

Such an inquiry, however, is outside the scope of this little work, and we can go no further into the matter than briefly to state and discount all contingent and complicating factors, in order the more quickly to get at fundamental principles.

There were, no doubt, many contingent factors aiding Buddhism at its start; such as the personality and genius of its founder, the devotion, zeal and organizing ability of his chief disciples or Theras, and the fresh, untainted vigour and moral example of the majority of the young fraternity. To preach and to live a life, in the eye of the public, of uncompromising and consistent righteousness and active benevolence, can never fail to carry weight, whatever be the philosophy and the logic of the underlying principles. Greater still is the effect, if the ethical vitality of the age is being sapped by a decadent ritual involving sacrificial butchery, caste-privilege and vain repetitions. "If this river Achĭrăvătī," said the Buddha to two young Brahmin disciples, "were full of water even to the brim and overflowing, and a man with business to be done on the further bank should come up, and want to cross over; and standing on this bank, he should invoke the further bank, and say: 'Come hither, O further bank! come over to this side!'—Now what think you, Vāse*tth*a? Would the further bank of the river Achĭră-vătī, by reason of that man's invoking and praying, and hoping, and praising, come over to this side?

"In just the same way, Vāse*tth*a, do the Brahmins, versed in the Three Vedas, omitting the practice of those qualities which really make a man a Brahmin,[1] and adopting the practice of those qualities which really make men non-Brahmins, say thus: 'Indra, we call upon, Soma we call upon, Isāna we call upon, Pajāpati we call upon, Brahmā we call upon, we call, we call!' Verily, Vāse*tth*a, that these Brahmins, by reason of their invoking and praying and hoping and praising, should after death become united with Brahmā—verily such a condition of things can in no wise be."[2]

The immolation of beasts in religious rites was first straitly condemned by Buddhists and Jains, but their denunciation gave voice to a feeling among the more spiritually-

[1] *Brahma* means excellent, holy.

[2] *Dialogues*, i. 309 ff.

minded in India, which, till they spoke, had but deprecated the institution in terms parallel to the "I will have mercy and not sacrifice" of the Hebrew prophets.[1]

And the frequency with which we find the Buddha consulted on the growing social claims of the Brahmins, shows that these claims were a burning question of the day. His own position, tracing the origin of social divisions or "castes" to some primitive norm or standard (*dhamma*) arising through division of labour, and recognizing only an aristocracy of intellect and virtue, must have appealed strongly to those who were dissatisfied with the Brahmins' assumptions.[2]

Let us now imagine the more intellectual hearers discounting these aspects of the new movement :—(*a*) devotion to a great and good personality and to his elect helpers ; (*b*) belief that, either in joining the religious fraternity, or in ministering to it as laymen, future ills might be averted, and (*c*) acceptance of a teaching as saving truth because the wise and good taught it. We may further imagine (*d*) the social and political reforming protest discounted :—the protest against sacerdotal and caste privilege and pretension, and the growing sense, during the temporary respite from war and invasion, of kinship and sympathy, together with the growth of traffic and intercourse ; all of which are prominently represented in early Buddhist literature.

[1] *Dialogues* i. 164 ff. [2] *Ibid.* i. 96 ff.

Yet again, we may discount, for such minds, (*e*) the more religious aspect of the movement:—the ethical revival demanding righteousness of life and inward piety in place of a relatively immoral and half-outgrown ritualism, and the sanction, to such piety and conduct, of a real present salvation open to all, irrespective of birth or sex.

Finally, in considering the survival of Buddhism down to the present day, we have to remember that, in common with other cults which have been propagated far and wide, Buddhism, where it prevailed, annexed as much as it was annexed. Where it was adopted, it also adapted itself. Thus, more thinly spread in some countries, both in the past and at the present day, and co-existing in a more or less illogical fusion with other cults, the moral sanctions of the latter may weaken and obscure the force of the moral sanctions in Buddhism. Hence we have to make allowance for (*f*) this adulteration in motives due to a mixture of creeds.

What then was the residual, distinctively Buddhist moral principle, which could appeal to disinterested and thoughtful adherents at the outset of the movement, and can appeal now to all? Here is a creed, depending on no revelation of the will or design of divine law-givers, nor on any human fiat whatever as the source of authority, and yet strenuously maintaining the truth and necessity of moral obligation, both during and after this life.

What is the basis of the sincere and genuine Buddhist's morality? What place does he find for "I ought," "I ought not?" What is his criterion of good and of bad conduct? And can he find in the cosmos the working of a justice, so far transcending man's puny efforts in that direction, as to make it worth any man's while to pursue good, and avoid bad?

Let us take the last inquiry first. The injustice and cruelty so often apparent in the natural course of things, the condemnation of nature at the tribunal of ethics:—this, as Huxley wrote, is a commonplace of all literatures. Is the Buddhist to follow good and flee from wickedness with only the order of nature to supplant Providence? "Why," might he not say, "was this child born a hunchback?" Does he hold that moral judgments—"This is just. That is unkind"—are merely the ethical creations of the human mind, reflecting on the general cosmic order of which it is a factor? And does he therefore say: "There's nothing good or bad but thinking makes it so"? Or does he find, in Huxley's words, a sanction for morality in the ways of the cosmos? [1]

Now it is only in systems where all things are derived from a creative One, that the *creation* of a moral order is ascribed to a pristine

[1] *Evolution and Ethics* (Romanes Lecture), the most remarkable contribution of any lay-student to the philosophy of Buddhism.

agency so conceived. We see it in the Semitic utterance: "I am the Lord and there is none else. I form light and create darkness; I make peace and create evil. . . . Let the skies pour down righteousness; let it spring up. I the Lord have created it." By implication, if not by utterances so sharply etched as this, the all-soul of Vedântism stands in a similar position. But in the Bhagavad-Gītā, the poem of a somewhat later age, we find a lesser claim put forward for divine providence in the person of the exalted one or Bhagavā. "When right is declining, and wrong increasing, . . . then, to protect the good and destroy evil-doers, and to confirm the right am I in every age of mankind reborn."[1] But to produce actions and to connect acts and their consequences, "here (only) nature (*prakriti*) works."[1]

Now the Pitakas do not assert, but they leave it clear enough, that, in the organic universe, right and wrong, and those consequences of actions which we call justice, retribution, compensation, are as truly and inevitably a part of the eternal natural or cosmic order as the flow of a river, the process of the seasons, the plant from the fertile seed. Going farther than the modern scientific standpoint, they substituted a cosmodicy for a theodicy, a natural moral order for the moral design of a creative deity.

This order which Buddhism saw in the

[1] *Bhag. Gītā*, iv. 8; v. 14.

universe was called in Pali *niyăm'ă*, that is, going-on, process. In it five branches, strands, phases were discerned :—*kamma-niyama*, order of act-and-result; *utu-niyama*, physical (inorganic) order; *bīja-niyama*, order of germs, or seeds (physical organic order); *chitta-niyama*, order of mind, or conscious life; *dhamma-niyama*, order of the norm, or the effort of nature to produce a perfect type. This fivefold synthesis does not occur in the Pitakas.[1] In them we have the expressions *niyāmatā*, *dhammatā*, abstract terms for normal orderly procedure. And each of the five kinds of process is taught severally. But the synthesis itself was made in or before Buddhaghosa's time (fifth century A.D.), or by himself.[2] He brings it forward when he is commenting on a refrain in the Buddha-legend, the telling of it being put in the mouth of the Buddha himself. The refrain is: "This, in such a case, is the norm" (or order of events, *dhammatā*,). And he illustrates each of the five phases thus :—(1) by the desirable and undesirable results following good and bad action, respectively; (2) by the phenomena of winds and rains; (3) by rice produced from rice-seed, or again, by sugary taste resulting from sugar-cane or honey; (4) by conscious processes, quoting from the Abhidhamma-Pitaka (*Patthāna*) :—" Antecedent states of consciousness with their

[1] Unless the two yet unedited Niddesa books reveal it.

[2] See *Dialogues*, ii. 8 *n*.

properties stand to posterior states with their properties in the relation of efficient cause." For instance, "in sense-cognition, the receptive and other phases of consciousness come to pass after, and because of, the sensation of sight."; (5) by the natural phenomena occurring at the advent of a Bodhisat in his last rebirth, *i.e.*, of one who, when adult, will become a saviour of the world, or Buddha. Hence we may define the *dhamma-niyama* as the order of things concerned with the production by the cosmos of its perfect or norm type. And we may say that our notion of moral law is covered by the first and last branches of the fivefold order, namely, the why we should be good, by the *kamma-niyama*, and the why we try to better our good, by the *dhamma-niyama*.

The first, or Kamma-order, expresses the universal fact that certain kinds of acts—bodily, vocal, mental—inevitably bring pain, both to the doer and to his fellows, while certain other kinds of acts bring pleasure or happiness to both. The ancient books did not trouble themselves very much to divide self sharply from others, and discuss egoism and altruism as has been done in modern ethics. Our present ideal of a conscious solidarity needed this preceding wave of conscious individualistic discrimination. Old-world wisdom felt rather than thought how *solidaires* all were one of another. The good man, in the Suttas, pursues the interests of both himself and others :—

> Ubhinnam attham carati ; attano ca parassa ca.[1]
> (He seeks the good of both—of others and of self.)

And to be and to do good consisted in refraining from injury, and bestowing happiness to the doer, in some form, at some time.

Buddhism claimed to reveal no original morality, nor any new rewards or punishments. Be good, it declared, and you will be reborn happily, as god, that is, as celestial being or angel, or, it may be, again as human. Be bad, and you will be reborn to misery, as an animal, as ill-plighted shade, or in the woes of purgatory. But think not that profession or ritual, sacrifice or prayer is part of goodness. There is no goodness save being harmless to, actively good to, your fellow-beings—human, and non-human. And there is no other certain sanction of goodness beyond the driving force of pain waiting on immoral living, and the pleasures rewarding moral living, now or in the long run. No sanction of an external will, divine or corporate, is quoted. Sayings of the Buddha are abundantly quoted to clench arguments on doctrine. But when the saints, in their poems, end the story of salvation won with the refrain: "Done is the Buddha's bidding!" the term used is not that for a despot's order: *āna*, but that for the instructions of a teacher: *sāsana*.

[1] *Samyutta-Nikāya*, i. 162, 222.

Now there was no need of inspired communications to teach mankind *that* they should avoid pain and pursue happiness. The teacher could aid mankind in connecting the bad and the painful, the good and the pleasant. They could claim, through higher insight, or through knowledge of orthodox tradition, to reveal ulterior connections beyond this life. But these connections and that insight were both of them integral parts of the cosmic order or norm of things. And when once the belief, that the *kamma-niyama* was as certain as the *bīja-niyama*, the deed done no less sure as a cause than the fertile seed sown, was become part of tradition's very marrow, then was there no need of a moral law or doctrine to be super-imposed from without upon the natural law of the universe. Sequence of deed and effect was as natural, as necessary, as *inexorably*, inevitably sure, as the way of sun and moon, the dying of all that is born, the reaction of sentience to stimulus.

Here then is where we need to think of what Buddhists think, and not of something else, if we would understand. You others, the Buddhist might say, invert the order of truth as we understand it; you assign rewards and punishments for certain acts and abstinences, calling this justice. But it is from the natural law or norm of things, wherein you say that you often see injustice, that you first learn what retribution is, and what is reward, such as we conceive in our *kamma* order. If you will study this order, you will see that there is no scheme of man-made justice which can stand comparison with the norm inherent in the universe—with the *dhammatā* of things. As surely as water, drawn up from earth and ocean by the sun re-descends as rain, so surely will a good, that is, a felicific act yield, somewhere and some-when, its happy results to the doer :—

> According to the seed that's sown,
> So is the fruit ye reap therefrom.
> Doer of good will gather good,
> Doer of evil evil reaps.
> Sown is the seed, and thou shalt taste
> The fruit thereof.[1]

The verse is the summary of a fable in a group of legends incorporated in a Pitaka book, and fathered as discourses on the Buddha. Yet, though popular in form, it presents accurately enough the substance of numerous passages inculcating the same doctrine in other words. And the acceptance of a Buddha's mission to teach a positive doctrine of act and consequence; in a word, of Karma, is, as we saw in the preceding chapter, one of the most emphatic statements imputed to Gotama.

This acquiescence of the Indian mind in the certainty of the natural law of Karma and also in the austere equity of it, is a notable feature for the Western religious mind to contemplate. For the idea of natural justice

[1] *Samyutta-Nikāya*, i. 227.

in life and destiny has not commanded the general confidence of mankind. The loyal and pious interpretation even of a theodicy or divine justice often tries the faithful. "Lord, who did sin, this man or his parents, that he was born blind?"

We might say: the parents, thinking of the working, we so little as yet understand, though we accept it, of heredity. So did the Jews, "thinking of something else," namely, of divine retribution stretched forth "even to the third and fourth generation of them that hate thee."

Buddhism would say: "The man had sinned." Afflictions, whatever disciplinary purge and preparation they afford by the way, are for Buddhists so many forms, not of pre-payment, by which future compensation may be claimed, but of settlement of outstanding debts, debts accruing from bad, that is to say, from evil-bringing, unhappiness-promoting acts—acts done either in this life, or, as in this born-blind's case, in previous lives.

Now this opens up other cases where we are always "thinking of something else." But a word more on this natural justice theory. Our ethical books, as we know, divide ethical systems into such as are Utilitarian or Dependent (systems which make the goodness of an act depend on its results), and Intuitionist or Independent ethics—systems which say we know instinctively or intuitively quite apart from results, whether acts of thought or deed are good or bad. Buddhism is at first sight Utilitarian. There is nothing either good or bad but result shows it to be so; results, that is to say, as *felt*; felt as giving pleasure or pain. Listen to the Buddha admonishing his only son, who was a bhikkhu: "Is there a deed, Rāhula, thou dost wish to do, then bethink thee thus:—Is this deed conducive to my own harm, or to others' harm, or to that of both, then is this a bad deed entailing suffering. Such a deed must thou surely not do." And so on for the opposite case.[1] Again, when inquirers ask the Buddha for a criterion of truth to judge between different gospels preached to them, he refers them to their own judgment as to the moral consequences likely to ensue if a certain gospel is followed: "Is it good, blameless, commended by the wise, conducive to happiness and welfare, or the reverse?"[2] This is utilitarian morality

But in that Buddhism believes in natural law or justice, whereby acts bring their own reward or punishment, not only to mankind but to the doer—whether human justice find him out or not—a natural justice which goes on inevitably and invariably constant, fulfilling itself it may be through human justice, but *always* fulfilling itself—a law not to be suspended by God, Buddhas, or man—in this belief Buddhists are Intuitionists. Or

[1] *Majjhima-N.*, i. 415. [2] *Anguttara-N.*, i. 190.

rather, they have made a vast induction similar to the great induction in their—and our—law of causation; and this induction is of course founded on a *belief*. This belief is, that what they see happening around them happens everywhere and always—the belief, namely, that the righteous act brings to the doer happiness, the wicked act, unhappiness.

We think of something else as the source of justice, and not the natural order of things. We think of justice as superimposed from without, analogous to our man-made laws, rules and conventions, coupled with an innate or acquired sentiment in our hearts or consciences.

But we can see that, for the thoughtful Buddhist, the *kamma-niyama* will have furnished as pressing a motive for moral conduct as if he held that an omniscient lawgiver watched and rewarded his acts. We see also that, when we say "injustice of nature," and speak of compensation hereafter as divine justice, we are thinking of explaining everything by (1) this life, and (2) future life, only. The Buddhist is thinking of the third great factor or *tertium quid*—he is thinking of the immense *past*, and how natural justice as to that past is working itself out here and now.

But before we consider the law of Karma in this wider Indian perspective, it will be well to pause, briefly to consider the word itself. For great is the Myth of the Word

But haziness of meaning is not favoured by Buddhism.

Kamma, or Karma—if we take the Sanskrit form more familiar to us—is literally doing, making, work, action.

To take dictionary instances :—*ayo-kamma* is iron-work; it is his "work" (*kamma*) that makes the peasant a peasant, the king, a king; minding one's own "business" (*kamma*); this is the "doing" (*kamma*) of those blind old folk, and so on. It is as well to note these instances. The Western mind, in retaining the use of the alien word "karma," has tended to see the meaning in a glamour, and to attach to it a mystic import which it would not convey to a Buddhist. Karma has even been made to cover an identical, permanent "somewhat," used to do duty for the soul, repudiated in Buddhism, as that which transmigrates from one life to another.

This "heresy" is of course only perpetrated when the work, act, or doing is considered with respect to such results as it may have; and when these results are expressed in terms of feeling and of ethical regard. Action so considered we usually term conduct, and the disposition to such action we call character. Morals or moral action, or ethical action covers both conduct and character. In Pāli the one word *kamma* does duty for all aspects of doing, making or action. Hence it covers all that we include in the phrase "thought, word and deed"—a threefold summary that we also meet with in the Zendavesta, and into which the Pitakas often divide the moral implication of the word "kamma."

The historical interest in the Buddhist attitude regarding acts and their results lies in the fact that this attitude constitutes an evolution of a theory contained in the germ in one of the older Upanishads. In the other older Upanishads, references to any theory of *karman* and its consequences in the doer's destiny are scarce and reveal no emphasized doctrine.[1] But in the Brihadāranyăka Upanishad, the references to moral action, though still very scarce, are very significant in their bearing on Buddhist doctrine. A man, we read, *is* as he behaves, and *will become* according as he behaves.[2] In other words the reality of a human being is not a static body or soul, but his character. Again, in another section, we read a man becomes good by good work, bad by bad work; *i.e.*, action or conduct.[3] This is the reply to the question put to a teacher of the Veda: "*Where* is a deceased person, when at death his body is dissolved into the elements, his mind gone to the moon?" *What* he is, is said to be "name," which "is endless, and

[1] E.g. *Kaushītakī Up.*, S.B.E., i. 277. *Chāndogya Up.*, *ib.* 130.

[2] *Ibid.*, xv. 176.

[3] *Ibid.*, p. 127.

by which he gains the endless world." (It is noteworthy that "name" is not superseded here by *ātman*. This, rendered as breath by Max Müller, goes into space. The Vedântist commentator renders it here as the cavity of the heart, the "seat" of the soul.) This reply is given secretly by the teacher, who takes his questioner apart: "let this question not be a public matter." Hence this doctrine of karma was either considered advanced and esoteric, or a trifle heretical. It does not anyway prove this portion of the Upanishad to be pre-Buddhistic. The doctrine openly and emphatically taught in the Pitakas is here tentatively touched upon. More cannot, in these limits, be said, save this: that in this and the Kaushītakī Upanishad, it is also stated that a man's knowledge as well as his deeds determine his future destiny. This twofold category is not Buddhist. We find mainly the threefold category of action by overt deed, by speech, and by volition (that is, action of purpose, intention, motive, will), as the determinants of man's destiny.

Let us now revert to the Buddhist perspective of the operation of karma, taking unceasing heed that we are not "thinking of something else." Consider the Buddhist idea of the relation of individuals to their acts or karma. "Beings," the Buddha is said to have taught, "are owners of their works (*kamma*), heirs of their works; their works are their matrix; their works are their lineage, and by their works are they established."[1]

Beside this place our traditional idea of the relationship: "Blessed are the dead that die in the Lord from henceforth. Yea, saith the Spirit, that they may rest from their labours, and their works do follow them." In this verse the idea of works is that of a train of attendant witnesses, gone before or after the transmigrating soul to testify to its deserts. In the former passage, the Buddha is replying to the question: "How do you account for the inequalities in the lot and circumstances of the sons of men?" Now the metaphors in the reply are very strong, establishing the most intimate connection between me and what I do, "and what," the Buddhist adds, "I have done in a former birth." We must never forget this, when reading them by the light of our own tradition. The nearest verse to the Buddhist belief is that modern line, quoted first years ago by Rhys Davids: "*And what we have been makes us what we are.*" My past works, says the Buddhist, were the matrix, the origin, the womb and the determinant of me, as are my present works of what I shall be. I have acted, and the effect, a transmitted composite resultant force, no less than is the electric current, is this "I," some one, that is to say, who is identical with that former "me" in the only sense in which Buddhism admits of identity.

[1] *Majjhima-N.*, iii. 203. "Beings," *i.e.*, *all* living things.

Here again we think of identity not wholly as Buddhists think. Buddhists, let it be remembered, were the co-founders (with the Jains) of Indian logic, a logic which can hold its own with ours. Let us therefore pause and consent not, if we hear them lightly accused of being illogical. We have certain so-called Laws of Thought, of which Aristotle said: Deny them, and you are a vegetable!—an unintelligent organism. One is the Law of Identity, formulated as A = A, or everything must be identical with, or the same as, itself. This is a useful convention in artificial transactions with specific, selected data, such as mathematics, legal or commercial contracts, etc. Validity there depends upon the meaning attaching to specific words, remaining unaltered. Looking away from conventions to the nature of things, we see how inexact is our use of "same." We use it for "identical" and for "similar." But in our organisms including consciousness, and in nature we find no such thing as identity. We are daily different, and everything not ourselves is changing also, slowly or quickly. History cannot "repeat itself," since every event leaves us changed; hence, if "it" recurs, altered characters and environment take part in it. "Same weather as yesterday" means a congeries of similars in the heavens and on earth. We cannot, therefore, formulate natural identity as A = A. It works out as $A = Ab = Ac = Ad = \ . \ . \ . \ A^n$. And at some moment, A*x*, we shall write, not A anything, but B, because A*x* has become so different from A, that we have what seems a fresh datum. Thus one day in our child's life, she ceases to be "baby"; she is now a girl! In these ever-changing sequences the Absolutist refuses to see any ultimate reality, substance or being. But Buddhism sees no other reality in them but this fact of change, or of becoming.

Another "something else" that hinders our understanding the Buddhist view is, that we do not take a sufficiently biological or organic view of their theory of change, becoming or causation (the three notions for them are inseparable). When we contemplate a changing "I" or self, we are too apt to picture a substituted something, like the fresh picture thrown upon a "magic" lantern screen, say, of the king at four years old and the king at forty. But we know that if we could have turned a ceaseless cinematograph on the king during that interval, we should witness a very gradual biological change. On no particular day would it be a different person that was presented, nor would it be identical with the presentation of a former or subsequent film. It would be that of something evolving, of a past that was at a given present instant creating, or *handing itself on to*, a future. We say: "I cannot be said to live hereafter unless I am I—remain I." The Buddhist says: "There is no 'same I,' *i.e.*, identical I, even during one life, during even two consecutive days of one life, much less in two successive planes of being." Truer than either assertion: "Everything is," "nothing is," is the view: "One thing happens from and because of another." Again he will say, "our Buddha said that, 'easier to the uneducated average man is self-conquest and self-emancipation with respect to the body, than with respect to consciousness, mind or cognition. For he can see how this four-elemental body has a beginning and a disintegration, is assumed and then surrendered. But with respect to mind, for ever is the uneducated ordinary man cleaving and devoted to, and affected by the notion that "this is mine, this I *am*, this is my self." Better were it if the uneducated ordinary man were to fix on the four-elemental body as the self than on mind. Why so? Because it is evident that this body persists for either a year or two up to even a hundred years or more. But that which is called consciousness and mind and intelligence, in the course of each night and day arises as one thing, ceases as another. Just as a monkey roaming in the forest clutches a branch, lets it go and clutches another, even like those varied clutchings of boughs is the procedure of consciousness, mind or cognition. Hence the educated Ariyan disciple thoroughly and fundamentally considers the causal order of things, namely that

"That being present, this comes to be; because that has arisen, this arises, etc." '[1]

We have to cast out from our imagination the view, untrue for Buddhism, that perpetual changing, or coming-to-be, going on in an individual, is a succession of *different individuals*. We have to substitute the notion of one individual evolving as we see other forms of life evolving about us. Consider this saying ascribed to the Buddha, which became a staple citation in later discussions:—"To say: *one* (person) acts, *another* reaps the fruit of those acts, is not true. And to say: *one and the same* both acts and is affected by the result is not true."[2] The Buddha's position, as he proceeds to state, is: "*I* teach a Midway between both extremes, to wit, the doctrine of Becoming by way of Cause." *We* should naturally say: one or the other of those former statements must be true. What then are we thinking of that differs from Buddhist thought?

Not the evolving life of essential change and becoming, but our own notion of identity, our own notion of mechanical causation, and, once more, our way of picturing the past episodes of what "I" did and said, and felt as so many pictures way-off in space, and in time pictured as space. But what if all those past "I"-pictures which we remember, ay, and those that we have forgotten, are still with and of us as part of the present composite

[1] *Samyutta-Nikāya*, ii. 94. [2] *Ibid.*, ii. 20.

notion we call, each of us, ourself? What if each self-experience, as it arose and passed, was wrought up into and became or evolved into, the next moment or phase of life? In this way, the present momentary self of each of us, is, if not the identical self of the past, the heir, outcome, product, resultant of the series, with all that series handed on and wrought up into it, no less than, to quote George Eliot's words, "the sunshine of past mornings is wrought up into the bloom of the apricot."[1]

This, any way, is more or less how the mediæval and modern Theravāda philosophy has unfolded that which it has judged to lie implicit or archaically expressed in the teaching of the Pitakas, such as I quoted from just now:—Not "the same," nor "another." And thus it is, that both the memory of a past self and the obligation to the future self is explained without the contradiction or the paralogism that critics charge Buddhism withal, and even adherents make excuses for. For it, the whole of the past is worked up into the present, ever handing on a *pacchăyă-satti,* that is, a causative influence, or force. Each successive phase of conscious life, therefore, "has all the potentialities of its predecessors and more."[2]

Thus Buddhism can greet a kindred spirit in Leibnitz's dictum: "The present is pregnant with the future," for with him, it

[1] *Adam Bede.* [2] S. Z. Aung, *op. cit.*, 42.

holds that "every phase of existence is a necessary outcome or evolution of what preceded it, and bears in it the seed of the future,"[1] thus translating the mechanical view of nature, not according to his theodicy, but according to its cosmodicy. Buddhists, too, can say with Henri Bergson: "Memory is no faculty for registering souvenirs. . . . There is no register, nor, strictly speaking, any faculty. . . . The heaping up of the past on the past goes on without intermission . . . following us at every moment. That which we have felt, thought, willed from infancy is here now, bending over the present moment which goes merging into it, pressing against the gate of consciousness which would leave it without." "Neither mechanical causality nor a final cause is an adequate translation of life."[2] Thus, the past self, as a memory, is wrought up into, and is part of, the present self, no less than the projected future self is a creation of the passing self that now is.

It were premature to do more than indicate the evolution, carried out in mediæval and modern Abhidhamma, of such theories. To make the records of this evolution accessible is a task of the near future. We may hope at no distant date to learn more of the fruitful working, in the collective Theravādin intelligence, of the original tenets of impermanence, non-self, and becoming or causation. But

[1] J. T. Merz, *Leibnitz* (1884), 177.

[2] *Evolution créatrice*, 5, 193.

we know enough to see clearly that for them, no less than for M. Bergson, the reality, the interest, of evolving phenomena lay in the transition or becoming, rather than in things viewed, for convenience' sake, as statical. They, too, before him, have been trying, " by an act of sympathy, to transport themselves to the inside of becoming."[1]

Let us now apply this Buddhist view of a self that never *is*, but is always *becoming*, *evolving*, to their forward view of natural justice in future lives.

Mention has been made of the pregnant old term, transmigration, wherewith it pleases the West to speak of the world-wide belief in life after death, when India is in question, although our own " passing hence " would be sufficiently synonymous. Most of us know of the logical fallacy imputed to Buddhism because it taught re-birth, and denied a " soul " to flit from birth to birth. It is quite true that, when we read the Pitakas, we seem to see a belief in transmigration of a passing soul, just as much as we see it in the books of animistic creeds. Some one dies, and " he " is re-born in such a new life. Or some saint gets supernormal memory and recollects, he will say, where " I " lived, and how, and as who. The Buddhists had new wine of their own, but there were only old bottles of phrases to hold the wine. So *we* still, as I have said, speak of the earth's movements in

[1] *Ibid.*, 177, 138, 338, 370, etc.

superannuated terms ; and of electrical energy in terms of a flowing and a striking, both of which are scientifically wrong ; and of ultimate security and certainty in terms of statics, of base and rest and stability, when in reality the most basic thing there is for us is motion, revolution in space. And Buddhists still spoke of rebirth *in terms* of animistic belief. "*It would be more correct,*" wrote Buddhaghosa, "*not to use popular modes of stating the case*"; as it is, "*we must just guard ourselves*" from supposing that these modes express fact.[1]

For let it not be supposed that the charge of being unintelligible and illogical is new to Buddhism. Since all the rest of India, *pace* the world, was animistically inclined, it was inevitable that the attack would start against the founder himself, and recur again and again. And ever we see that what the assailants needed in order to understand Buddhist doctrine, was insight into (1) impermanence of the self of any given moment ; (2) connection between that self and any past or future self through transmitted energy, or evolution. Let us show this in the books.

The Buddha is giving a lecture to his Order on *Anattā*, the absence of absolute or god-like soul in mind or body. And we read : " Then in the mind of a certain bhikkhu (he is unnamed) the idea arose : " If nothing in body or mind has, or is, soul (self, *attā*),

[1] See below, p. 145.

what soul is there to be affected by deeds which no soul has done ?" Now the Exalted One knew what was passing in that bhikkhu's mind. And he went on to address the brethren, saying: "Now it is possible, bhikkhus, that herein some futile person, who has not understood and is still ignorant, may, under the influence of craving, stray from the Teacher's doctrine and fancy: If nothing in body or mind has, or is, soul, what soul is there to be affected by deeds which no soul has done? But ye, bhikkhus, have been trained by me in causation, respecting various states under various conditions. What think ye then? Is body, is mind permanent or impermanent?" "Impermanent, lord." "Is that which is impermanent liable to suffering or not?" "It is liable, lord." "But is it proper to say, of that which is impermanent, liable to suffering and to change, This is mine; I am this; this is the soul of me"? "No, lord." [1]

The answer is to us as unexpected as the question is oddly framed. We should probably have used our more magisterial diction, and asked: "Is it possible, let alone just, to reward or punish a doer A in another life, when A has become so different that he can no longer be said to be A?" And anyway we should have hoped to find, in the reply, a systematized statement of eschatology, put in the mouth of the fountain-head of doctrine.

[1] *Majjhima-N.*, iii. 19 f.

That which actually is recorded is the sort of rebuke which in our logic might be used to meet the "fallacy of many questions," or the legal trap of a leading question, *e.g.* "Have you left off beating your wife?" The reply might be: "I am a bachelor." So here the reply is a catechism to show that there is no wife—no soul—as soul was currently conceived—to speculate about. Were men, or had men such a soul or self as the Indian *ātman*, the conditions of life, past, present and future, would necessarily be very different. "If the body, bhikkhus, or if the mind were the Self, it would not be subject to infirmities, and we should be able to say: "Let my body . . . or let my mind be such and such."[1] A permanent subject of bodily and mental phenomena could not logically be predicted of man as we here and now know him.

Thus the reply gives no fresh theory, but throws the questioner back on to first principles. Given:—the current conception of *ātman* or soul; the current belief in the infinite renewal of sentient life; the Norm doctrines of perpetual change, transitive becoming and natural moral order:—then the questioner finds himself landed in the Buddhist conclusion.

If it be objected that the perduring self or soul is not really an unchanging or divine entity, but is together with body and mind,

[1] *Vinaya Texts*, i. 100 (*Sacred Books of the East*, XIII.).

capable of growth, as of deterioration, " changing according to the nature of its deeds for better or worse," as Plato said, then this is not the aspect of animism rejected by Buddhism. This is clear from the usual form of argument, given above, by which the Ātmanistic soul-belief is refuted. But such a view, in Buddhist eyes, surrenders the essential soulship of soul, and reduces it to a sort of sixth khandha, or factor of that individuality which dissolves at each death, but which, as a sort of force set free, results in the birth and growth of a new individual. The Buddhists demurred only to anything that enters into, and is integral with, life as we know it, and yet is excluded from the law of becoming. If, in the midst of this law or order, wherein transient phenomena were ever being called up by transient antecedents, and causing others in their turn, we interpolate something that is not so called into being, but has a special nature of its own, we upset the order of the phenomenal universe by bringing in a new mystery, which explains nothing *in* that order save *from without.*

Let us now turn to the after-born systematizers, and watch their efforts to elucidate and keep intact the original mandate. First, the lucid, direct parables of Nāgasena in the *Milinda:*

" Sir," asks Milinda, " can there be rebirth where there is no transmigrating (passing on) ? " " Yes, sire, there is the former without the latter." "How can that be? Give me an illustration." "Suppose, sire, a man were to light a lamp from another lamp, can it be said that lamp transmigrates from lamp?" "Nay, sir." "And do you admit, sire, that when you were a boy, you learnt some verse or other from your teacher?" "Yes, sir, I do." "Well then, sire, did that verse transmigrate from your teacher?" "Nay, sir." "Even so, sire, is there rebirth without transmigration."[1]

Again, as to moral responsibility:—"Reverend Nāgasena," said Milinda, "what is it that is reborn?" "Mind and body, sire, are reborn." "What, is it this same mind and body that are reborn?" "Nay, sire, not so; but by this mind and body there is doing of deeds lovely or evil, and by these deeds (*kamma*) another mind and body are reborn." "If this same mind and body, sir, be not reborn, will one not become free from evil deeds?" The Thera replied: "If one were not reborn, one would become free from evil deeds, but inasmuch as one is reborn, one is not thus free." "Give me an illustration." "Suppose, sire, some man were to carry off another man's mango; and the owner accused him before the chief. And the thief were to say: 'Your honour! I have not carried off mangoes from this man. The mangoes he planted are not those that I picked.' Would he be guilty?" "He would." "On what

[1] *Op. cit.*, i. 71.

ground?" "Whatever he might say, he admits the former mango (as cause), becoming guilty by the latter mango (as effect)." "Even so, sire, one does deeds lovely or evil under this mind and body, and is thereby reborn, but not freed from the deeds that are evil."[1]

The king elicits six more illustrations from Nāgasena—a redundancy which points to the difficulty, or the importance of the doctrine, or to both. I give the last, because it is utilized by the later, more philosophic, less popular dissertation of Buddhaghosa.

"Suppose, sire, a man were to buy of a herdsman a pail of milk, and leave it in his charge till the morrow, by which time it had turned sour. And when he came to claim it, he were to say: 'It was not curds I bought of you; give me my pail of milk.' Now if they, disputing, appealed to you, sire, how would you decide?" "In favour of the herdsman." "But why?" "Because, in spite of whatever the buyer might say, the curds were derived from the milk." "Even so, sire, it is one mind-and-body that ends at death, another that is reborn, and yet, since this mind-and-body is derived from the former mind-and-body, it is not freed from the evil deeds (that went to produce it)."[2]

Now to Buddhaghosa's *Way of Purity*:—

[1] *Sacred Books of the East,* xxxv.; and passages in Warren's *Buddhism in Translations.*

[2] *Op. cit.,* i. 75.

"He who has no clear idea of death or of rebirth, and does not master the fact that death is the dissolution of the five factors (mind and body), and that rebirth is the appearance of the five factors, *he* concludes that 'A living entity deceases and transmigrates into another body,' or 'A living entity is reborn, and has got a new body.' . . . No elements of being transmigrate from the last existence into the present, nor do they appear in the present existence without causes in the past existence.[1] For, at the hour of death, . . . the last conscious act is as a man who, to cross a ditch, swings himself over by a rope hung on a tree above him. Yet he does not really alight,[2] for while the last conscious act dies away (and this is called passing away), another conscious act arises in a new life, and this is called rebirth, or conception. But it is to be understood that the latter conscious act did not come into the present life from the previous life. We must also understand, that it is only to causes contained in the old existence that its present appearance is due. . . . Now, if taking any continuous series, an *absolute sameness* obtained, then *e.g.*, sour cream could

[1] "Existence" in Pāli is literally "becoming" (*bhava*). They rejected the abstract word "being" (*atthitā*).

[2] I differ here slightly from Warren's reading of the Pāli. His rendering does not seem to be sufficiently intelligible. But the whole passage needs sounder scholarship than his or mine.

not arise from milk. And if there were *absolute difference*, the milk-owner could not get sour cream in the ordinary course of things. Hence *if we use popular phrases, we must guard ourselves from supposing that we have here absolute identity or diversity.* But some may say: if the husbandman ceases to be, he does not taste the fruit which he sowed; if there be no transmigration of mind and body, then will the fruit of one's acts be borne by a different thing from that which produced it. But I say: If you take that fruit *as arising in a series*, you get no absolute identity or diversity, so that we cannot say, the fruit is got by the same, nor by something quite different. We train the young, but it is in the adult that we look for the effects."

We see, then, that Buddhism, through its theory of becoming, claims to reconcile a position of scientific doubt regarding the origin and end of life with an emphatic repudiation of materialistic or nihilistic conclusions as to the apparent physical beginning and end of life, and with an equally emphatic affirmation of moral responsibility as coeval with life. Let us glance once more at the perspective.

Somehow and somewhen there arose between the religious philosophies with which we are more familiar, and those of India (not to speak of others), this dividing line of belief:—on the one hand belief in individual life commencing here and now, but perduring, as to one part of it, to infinity; on the other hand, belief in individual *living*, begun from, and lasting into, eternity, or at least for a very long time, perduring either in a sequence of perishable forms, or perduring without material re-embodiment. Buddhism, as a characteristically Indian movement, accepted the view of life here as a moment between two eternities, and as but one span of living in an infinite series of such spans. This series it pictures as a round or cycle (*vatta*) of continual movement (*samsāra*).

It envisages all becoming, all reaction of one state of things upon another, after an organic type of change, namely, as growth, equilibrium and decay, succeeded again by growth. The person ended; the living of him went on. For living is conceived as force, subdivided to an indefinite extent in individual tendencies or channels, conserved from everlasting, and actual, at any given moment, as organized beings (human, celestial, animal, etc.). The last mental or conscious act, just when the body is ceasing to act as the living nucleus *pro tem.*, is an act of transitive causation, like its predecessors. And it transmits its *pacchaya-satti*, or causal energy—so runs the hypothesis—to some newly conceived embryonic germ, human or non-human.

To answer the question: "In *which* new embryo does any given final flicker of mental *kamma* produce its effect?" no materials containing any Buddhist theories on the subject are as yet available, either mediæval or modern. And these pages are only concerned with such Buddhist theories as are a part of their philosophical tradition. Any scientific theorizing on the subject by Buddhists themselves can only claim attention in this part of the world as the outcome of genuine scientific inquiry. Meanwhile our own theories of heredity are still sufficiently inadequate to account for the facts of individual character and faculty, not to warrant our sweeping aside other theories as unworkable.[1]

Whatever be our own or others' vague hypotheses as to its origin, our conscious self, immaterial factor, soul, is, for most of us, something that is new, fresh, a thing of yesterday, a babe, of mushroom growth. Infinite, or at least indefinitely long-lived in one direction—the future—it starts with no definitely conceded background of past life. Our feeling with regard to its future has the pungent aggressiveness and intensity of youth. We feel we should like to "have it all over again," and do better. The Buddhist, with the vista of believing vision down a long past of one individualization after another, looks with maturer eyes at the flux of things and at the fluidity of his personal identity. He believes indeed that, were he of saintly purity

[1] *Cf.* the interesting article, "Transmigration," by Ananda Metteyya, in the review, *Buddhism* (Rangoon), I., 1903.

and wisdom, like the elect Theras and Therīs of old, he could remember many of his past phases of life; nay, he holds that, now and again, the fresh and untenanted mind of a child can remember—and be proved as remembering—persons and places in its own previous birth.[1]

And he might say to us: "Your balance-sheet seems to be somewhat one-sided. It is all debts here, future payment there; debts owing to you through natural injustice, handicapping by heredity, ill luck, etc., recompense for the same hereafter. But where is your entry of debts incurred by you in the past, which you by pain, trouble or failure, are now paying off? You are only less illogical when you keep in view 'original sin.' We think that, when now we suffer grief and pain, if only that life or living, which in the past created Me, had been less foolish, we should each of us be now much happier." Thus the Buddhist's view of his present activities has a wider basis, they being but one group of incidents in an indefinitely prolonged past, present and future series. They are, as has been said, no mere train of witnesses for or against him, but a stage in a cumulative force of tremendous power. He and his works stand in a mutual relation, somewhat like that of child to parent in the case of past works, of parent to child in the case of future works. Now no normal mother

[1] *Cf.* L. Hearn, *Gleanings in Buddha Fields*, p. 267 f.

is indifferent as to whether or how she is carrying out her creative potency. Nor can any normal Buddhist not care whether his acts, wrought up hourly in their effect into his present and future character, are making a happy or a miserable successor.

And so, without any definite belief as to how, or in what realm of the universe he will re-arise as that successor to his present self, the pious Buddhist, no less than his pious brethren of other creeds, goes on giving money and effort, time and thought to good works, cheerfully believing that nothing of it can possibly forego its effect, but that it is all a piling up of merit or creative potency, to result, somewhere, somewhen, somehow, in future happiness—happiness which, though he be altruistic the while, is yet more a future asset of *his*, than of some one in whom he naturally is less interested than in his present self. He believes that, because of what he is now doing, some one now in process of mental creation by him, and to all intents and purposes his future "self," will one day taste less or more of life's trials. To that embryonic character he is inextricably bound, ever making or marring it, and for it he is therefore and thus far responsible.[1]

[1] With the growth of the altruistic belief in transferring merit to another I have no space to deal.

CHAPTER VI

THE NORM AS IDEAL

In proceeding from theories underlying ideals to consider the ideals themselves, the conception of Dhamma as Norm affords an easy bridge. It was as natural and inevitable for Buddhist doctors to develop the import of such a notable term as Dhamma, as it was for Christian fathers to develop that of the equally notable term Logos. But while it is legitimate enough to group under Dhamma those central philosophical principles, on which the doctrine was based, the latter, under the aspect of a Norm, was an application of theories, held as true, to the will, and the expression of them in conduct. A norm resolves the contents of experience into a scale of values, and the things of topmost value into ideals.

Judgment of values according to the Norm or Dhamma is, in Buddhism, called Right-view or Perfect-view (*sammā-diṭṭhi*, i.e. *summa-doxa*, if, to give the European equivalents, such a hybrid compound be let pass). And such a view, views, or belief is placed, in a Buddha-discourse, in the forefront of the scheme of righteous conduct called the "Noble Eightfold Path," as being the determinant of "right intention" and of the remaining six right or perfect factors.[1]

In deciding what things this Right-view ranked as of supreme worth, the early literature of the Canon reveals, as compared with the scriptures of more familiar cults, so great a dissimilarity amid much that is similar, that the effect is baffling. On those who hold that norms, ethics, or religions approximate nearest to truth in such features as they have in common, the effect is also repellent and disheartening. It is the reverse on those who can appreciate the significance, for achievement and progress, in the differences of one tradition from another. The late, half paralyzed and wholly crippled Henry Warren, to whose indomitable spirit and vast industry English readers of Buddhist authorities owe so much, could write as follows: "A large part of the pleasure that I have experienced in the study of Buddhism has arisen from the strangeness of what I may call the intellectual landscape. All the ideas, modes of argument, even the postulates assumed . . . have always seemed so . . . different from anything to which I have been accustomed . . . they so seldom fit into Western categories."[2] This strangeness arises not only from what we find, but from postulates and

[1] *Majjh. N.* iii, 71 ff.

[2] *Buddhism in Translations*, p. 284.

standpoints that we miss. Here for instance are two of the latter :—

Buddhism, in the Dhamma of the Pitakas, puts aside a theodicy, or, let us say at once, a theistic position, and accepts a cosmodicy. The great wheel of cosmic order goes on, but it is *a-kāraka,* "without maker, without known beginning, continuing to exist by virtue of a concatenation of cause and effect."[1] As a notable movement of religious and ethical reform, Buddhism was not unique in being nontheistic. Jainism was no less so; so was the Sānkhya. But, without complicating our subject by dragging in these, we may search the Pitakas in vain for any expression, that to have turned away from the support and consolation of theism was felt as a conscious loss. Buddhists took up virtually the position of orphans "in the world's vast orphanage"—to borrow a phrase of W. D. Howells. But they do not labour under any manifested feeling of bereavement, such as lapsed Christians, inheriting a tradition of paternal theism, would inevitably feel. Sakkā, ruler of the nearer heavens, Brahmā, supreme in the remoter realms, "The Mighty One, The All-seeing One, Ruler, Lord of All, Controller, Creator, Ancient of Days, Father of all that are and to be,"[2] are mentioned with a cheerful courtesy when brought in as appreciators of the Master's wisdom. But

[1] Buddhaghosa, *Way of Purity,* xvii.
[2] *Dialogues,* i. 281.

irony replaces respect, when the question arises of their wisdom and knowledge being comparable to his. Nor is any note of loneliness and desolation heard when the more mystic, less anthropomorphic aspect of deity as Ātman is confronted. We may possibly think fit to read between the lines :—to include in the mode of suffering described as "separation from that which is dear," the rejection of a pantheistic rapture described in the Upanishads as "in Whom to dwell is happiness imperishable." But there is no positive evidence to warrant our doing so. Judged by such evidence, the Buddhist tone seems not that of mourning orphans, but that of legatees investing capital hitherto lying idle

There is another position absent from the Pitakas. No fear is expressed lest the stability of morals be upset through the gods being denied all creative and providential omnipotence. Are we going to keep the Commandments, if we see in the glory of those forty days and nights on Sinai a myth? is a present and pressing anxiety in Western discussion of animism. To quote one of the most recent: "I gravely doubt," writes Mr. McDougall,[1] "whether whole nations could rise to the level of an austere morality, or even maintain a decent working standard of conduct, after losing a belief in a future life and other positive religious beliefs." Now

[1] *Body and Mind! a History and a Defence of Animism,* xiv.

in the discourses of the Sutta-Pitaka, the rudiments of morality are put forward, with much repetition and emphasis, as the indispensable foundations of all good or desirable conduct, for both laity and fraternity. To abstain from taking life, not to take what is not given, sexual purity, to abstain from lying, abusive, slanderous or idle speech, to abstain from intoxicating drink—this fivefold code was termed *sīla*, that is to say, "habit," or *sŭ-char'ĭta*, good conduct. Habitual morality is compared to the broad earth, on which, as their fulcrum or basis, all creatures move, stand or rest; and again, *sīla* is compared to the sources of the great rivers and the ocean, starting as rill and burn way up in the mountains, and ministering to an increasing scale of animal growth as they descend and wax deep and wide, till merged in the ocean.[1]

Emphatic and uncompromising as is the position, in the Dhamma, of *sīla*, it is still only fundamental to right view and right living; it is not supreme. Here it is worth while to note a sequence in one of the more composite discourses, or grouped fragments of discourse, in the Suttas. Just after the Buddha has rebuked a bhikkhu for propagating, as sound doctrine, that there was no inherent retribution in the committing acts considered wrong, he is represented as calling morality (*dhamma* in conjunction with *a*-

[1] *Samyutta-Nikāya*, v. 46, 63, etc.

dhamma), merely a raft, serving a vital, but temporary, need :—

"Bhikkhus, I will teach you the Norm as symbolized by a raft, as something to escape by, but not to be clung fast to. Suppose a man come midway on his journey to a great sheet of water, beset as to its hither bank with many perils, but safe and secure as to its further shore, and to cross which nor ship nor bridge is there. But suppose that he takes grasses, brushwood and branches, and so binds together a raft, that thereon, toiling with hands and feet, he gains the further shore in safety. Now do you judge that he should, considering how greatly the raft had helped him, bear it along with him on his head and shoulders, or should be leave it stranded or floating, and go thence whither he wished? . . . Even thus, Bhikkhus, understand that ye must put away moral rules, let alone immoral rules."[1]

But as to any ulterior basis or motive being required for morality, the traveller's own great need is obviously considered as a sufficient reason, namely, the natural instinct of avoiding pain and pursuing happiness, in one word, of self-preservation. Whether under self, we mean himself, or include the social self or common human need, is really immaterial for the present argument. Moral conduct had borne mankind safely through the chaos of the unmoral and the immoral in

[1] *Majjhima-Nikāya*, i. 134.

social life. Human experience had tested the value of such vehicles. "The wise," who are so frequently referred to in the dialogues, approve of them. And therewith, as the German idiom says, all is said.

As believing in a cosmodicy, Buddhism, like the scientific position which believes in such no less, recognizes fully and promptly the facts of natural law, and of evolution. It exceeds the (more sceptical) scientific position by its inclusion of moral law in its cosmodicy. Herein it is more on the side of the Psalmist, in its view of the fate that, not merely probably, but inevitably befalls the wicked man, temporarily rivalling the green bay tree, and the righteous man temporarily reduced to beggary. Here, it says, are the facts. Goodness is necessarily profitable and advantageous. Badness is no less necessarily unprofitable and disadvantageous. You cannot kick against the pricks, or, as the Buddhist proverb says, crush in a mountain with a lotus, or chew iron with your teeth.

A certain degree of anxiety, nevertheless, as to the majority realizing the binding nature of moral responsibility, is no doubt present in Buddhist literature, and has been dealt with in the preceding chapter. It arose, not from the rejection of creative and over-ruling moral agency, but from the rejection of persistent, unchanging identity in the individual who was subject to moral law. Thus far, then, in the field of ideals and aspirations, the

Buddhist landscape is unfamiliar :—the rejected Over-soul is not consciously missed or regretted; and anxiety as to the source of instability in moral obligation is transferred from this rejected belief to the rejection of a popular belief concerning the soul of man.

When we consider the said landscape further, we cannot but be struck by the way in which the following after the ideal is very largely expressed in terms of getting rid of the unideal. The widest possible concept for the unideal, expressed by Christians in the word sin, is for Buddhists comprised in the word *dukkha* :—suffering, pain, ill, unhappiness—as the more truly ultimate term. Evil conduct was a cause of ill, but it was only evil conduct in virtue of its ill effects, now or in the long run. A utilitarian or experiential trend of thought cannot but throw emphasis on the consequences of conduct. And if consequences be brought forward, we come inevitably to consequences *as felt*, namely as happiness or as pain.

Now the emphasis laid in the Dhamma on the fact of Dukkha is very great, and has won for Buddhism such epithets as "pessimism pure and simple," with variations; and "the creed of a decadent epoch"; of an age, that is to say, undergoing a phase of social senility. It might perhaps, with equal truth, be said, that the very term "world-sorrow" (*Weltschmerz*) was coined by modern romantic literature to fit the violent obsessing misery, held to be a passing phase of the prime of youth. Such facile generalizing, however, is bound to become discredited, even in the case of Buddhism, as our knowledge grows. The former view, for instance, was put forward, in days preceding Pāli research, emphatically and dogmatically by Orientalists, who held themselves bound, for some reason or other, to vindicate, at the expense of Buddhism, the established faith of the majority of their readers. Barthélemy St. Hilaire, after inveighing against the "incurable désespoir" of Buddhism, concludes thus: "The sole but immense service which Buddhism may render us, is, by its sad contrast, to make us appreciate still more the inestimable value of our beliefs, by showing us what it has cost humanity not to share in them."[1] Of this attitude, so dear to the popular exponent, so unworthy of the scholar, Max Müller, in reviewing the book, could say: "in the body of the work he never perverts the chair of the historian into the pulpit of the preacher!"[2] A similar standpoint was taken a quarter of a century later, by Monier Williams in his popular lectures, in which those aspects of Christianity which he judged most congenial to his readers, are contrasted with the "ultra-pessimistic view," "the extinction of desires," the "inaction and apathy," typical, according to him, of Buddhism.

[1] *Le Bouddha et sa religion*, 1862, p. 182.
[2] *Edinburgh Review*, 1862, Essays II., p. 187.

When we turn from works by specialists written from this peculiar standpoint, to those of a more general character on the history of thought, it is not surprising to find such hardy perennials transplanted. Max Müller's review of St. Hilaire is quoted by Dr. Sully in his scholarly *Pessimism, a History and a Criticism* (1877, 1892), as a warrant for calling Buddhism " pessimism, pure and simple."

To this work we will presently return. The undoubted emphasis on ill as a ground wave in the rhythm of life is shared by Buddhism to some extent with Jainism and the Sānkhya system. That all three systems rejected the theistic standpoint *may* be causally connected with this emphasis. And it may, again, be here that we find, deeply pervading, if not consciously accounted for, that sense of loneliness and orphanhood which seemed to be missing.

That such systems as these should face the grim realities of life, and find Ill the first most prominent fact, is only natural. But it is Buddhism alone that made Ill the systematized point of departure for its practical philosophy. " Just this have I taught and do I teach," the Buddha is recorded as saying: " ill, and the ending of ill (*dukkhañ c'eva dukkhassa nirodhañca*)."[1] In the legend of the Buddha[2] the cardinal *dukkha*-facts of

[1] *Majjhima-Nikāya*, i. 140.

[2] *Dialogues*, ii. 18.

life arrest like the crash of opening chords in a tragic symphony: Sickness, Age, Death, each seen in succession for the first time—as by every young creature they are seen, when the significance of them first grips his heart. And with the problem of ending them the chief theme opens: "Verily this world has fallen upon trouble, with its births and ageing and dying, and rebirths," ponders the Buddha-about-to-be; "and from this suffering no man knoweth any way of escape. O, when shall a way out from this suffering, from decay and from death, be made known!" And the second theme makes response: Through natural causes arises suffering; wholly to end it suppress the causes. In your own human hands lies the remedy.

It is sometimes maintained by Vedântists, that every ethical doctrine in Buddhism is anticipated in Vedântist literature, literature, that is to say, belonging to the Vedic tradition. This is in a sense perhaps true, but true only on a level with similar sayings, that one may find everything that affects all mankind mentioned in the Bible, in Dante, in Shakespeare. It is only what may be called structural treatment, and structural emphasis, that counts. Incidental allusions may contain mention, but cannot be said to emphasize. Relatively speaking, the fact and significance of suffering, like the fact and significance of the law of causation and karma, are, in those Upanishads, which are generally considered pre-Buddhistic, incidental allusions only.

The words *duhkha, artta* (suffering and sorrow) occur about fifty times in Jacob's *Concordance of the Principal Upanishads and Bhagavad Gītā.* As compared with the occurrence of such terms in the Pitakas, this sum is a mere trifle. An incidental testimony to the absence of emphasis, in such occurrences of the tragic terms as there are, is afforded by the significant absence of them from the indexes to works on the Upanishads! Nor are the terms leading features in a principal theme. Moreover, barely one-fourth of the references occur in the older Upanishads. That they occur for the most part, together with the references to karma and causation, only in the obviously later Upanishads, forms a strong presumption that these were compiled under the influence, not only of Sānkhyan thought (this is textually admitted) but also of Buddhist (and possibly also of Jainist) thought.

The Upanishads are mystical. And the mystic tends to be optimistic. It must be no small bliss to realize that the highest spirit, who is all bliss, absolutely free, is none other, really, than your own self or soul.

Now, with respect to the getting rid of the Un-ideal, or of Dukkha, there is, in the original Buddhist attitude towards the perponderance and predominance of pain, a sensitive irritability and revolt that cannot be reconciled with pessimism pure and simple. There is no resignation to a common inevitable doom. The natural instinct to avoid pain and to make for its opposite is encouraged. I do not mean that particular painful experiences were not to be patiently endured. "Suffer it to be so, O Arahant, suffer to it be so," the Buddha is represented calling to a persecuted disciple who comes to him with broken head and streaming wounds, "you are *now* feeling results of your karma that might have cost you centuries of suffering in purgatory." The disciple had been a notorious brigand, converted by the Buddha, and former victims were taking their revenge on him. Again a general admonition by the Buddha runs as follows: "Thus, bhikkhus, must ye train yourselves to meet no matter what treatment at men's hands: Our mind shall not be perverted, nor shall we utter evil words, but we shall abide friendly and compassionate, our thoughts affectionate and not hostile; and we shall continue to suffuse that person with heart of love, and so . . . too, the entire world with heart of love, rich and sublime, and boundless, free from anger or malevolence."[1]

All particular experiences of *dukkha* had been incurred by one's own past karma, and belonged to the natural justice of the world's order. But the chastening rod was not kissed on that account. To call the heart of

[1] *Dialogues*, i. 127; *cf.* Oldenberg, *Buddha* (5th ed.), 255.

the Sutta Pitaka the cry of outraged humanity, ravaged by that fearful rod, were to exaggerate, but not to an excessive degree. It recognizes fortitude under suffering, but the welcoming of pain as a discipline is not in its scheme of salvation. In it the eyes and the heart of the Indian conscience are shown opened to the groaning and travailing of sentient life as they never were before. The optimistic and complacent moonlight reveries of Ātmanism are shattered, and a chill dawn of daylight values has crept up. Life, as it actually is, is felt to be intolerable, a thing to be mended or ended.

To call revolt rather than resignation the Buddhist standpoints over against the ills of life, is nothing new. But since the latter word is often used on topics Buddhistic, it is as well to distinguish. The following citations reveal a spirit that cannot be called characteristically Buddhist: "Whosoever doth not bear his cross . . . cannot be my disciple" (Luke xiv. 27). "Lord, we pray not for tranquillity, nor that our sorrows may cease . . ." (Savonarola). "It is a blind self-seeking which wants to be freed from the sorrow wherewith the whole creation groaneth and travaileth" . . . (G. Eliot in *Adam Bede*). And we have only to contrast the typical presentations of the two persons, each of whom has been called "Light of the World," to realize deep-lying differences in the aspect of an ideal.

To see Dukkha pervading life, and to revolt and seek how to put an end to it, may not be the opposite of pessimism, but it is less "pessimism pure and simple" than seeing and resigning oneself. Now whereas a widely accepted gospel which is purely and only pesimistic is impossible, not to say, inconceivable, it may well be maintained that no great gospel can have any but a pessimistic point of departure :—"Hear, O sons of men, evil is life!" The test of pessimism is rather to be sought in the value attached by the gospel to the possibilities in the life that is thus marred by evil. Is the gospel's way of escape from evil, from the un-ideal, realizable in and through life? If not, then such a gospel is not necessarily pessimism pure and simple, but it is not optimistic as to the possibilities of life.

Let us revert to Dr. Sully's book. Interpreting the terms, pessimism and optimism, "in their widest meaning," the author takes them to mean that "life has no value, or has value respectively"; is "unworthy, unsatisfying, lamentable," or the opposite. And the ground on which Buddhism is called pessimism by Dr. Sully is authorized by Max Müller's statement, that its view of life had no such happy "solution" as was offered by the opposed beliefs of Brahmanic Pantheism. That happy solution entailed an unearthly and unknown renewal of existence after this life. The real theme and nucleus, however, of Dr. Sully's book, comes to this: that the positive value of life increases, rather than diminishes, with a belief in its evanescence.

Here is an estimate of life, as not depending for all its value on pantheistic or other solutions, judged by which the pessimism imputed to Buddhism may need further modification. Among recent imputings to this effect, Dr. Saleeby, in *The Survival Value of Religion*,[1] wiped out a future for Buddhism on the ground that it was "mere pessimism," *i.e.*, "since it preaches the worthlessness of life," the contention of the essay being that, to have a high survival value, a religion must enhance the value of life, taken in quality, if not in quantity.

This conclusion would seem to merit general acceptance. But the claim for Buddhism may also be accepted, that it is a remarkable exemplification of that conclusion. The Dhamma, to begin with, has already shown a very fair power of survival, exceeding that of nearly every other creed. And it enhances, perhaps more than any creed, the value of life, when life is not taken in breadth and length, but when a special quality of life is selected.

This may not seem obviously true. But if we consult the two main ideals of life in early European culture, the Greek and the Christian, we find in both, that the life on which high value was set, is very restricted indeed in

[1] *Fortnightly Review*, 1906.

breadth. As to life considered in length, that is, as prolonged beyond the grave, the Christian solution is much more pronounced in its estimate than the Greek. Nevertheless, even for it, there is an indefinite restriction in breadth. "Many are called, but few are chosen."

We are accustomed to picture the ancient Greek, living within a certain epoch of florescence, as reckoning his earthly life well worth having. We note his delight in physical culture, social functions, intellectual inquiry, and artistic beauty. And we think of him dreading the dim shades of the after life in the mood interpreted in Swinburne's *Atalanta* :

> I am gone down to the empty, weary house,
> Where no flesh is, nor beauty, nor swift eyes,
> Nor sound of mouth, nor might of hands and feet.

Advance in archæology, however, and even in literary research, has revealed to us phases of the ancient Greek temperament neglected before :—evidences of aspiration after a blessed future with the gods, longings to escape (expressed in the very metaphor used in India by Buddhists) "from the painful, misery-laden wheel" of birth and of fate. But there appears no definitely conceived ideal of meliorism for humanity in this life. The golden age is behind. The ideal republic is the dream of an individual genius. Nor was the quality of life, such as was held to be here desirable, conceived as widely distributed.

The slave and the wife were civically of small account. With regard to the majority in the state, past, present and future, the Greek estimate of life may be said to have been pessimistic. The opposite view held only respecting a certain quality of mundane life, such as the fortunate (mainly male) minority might live.

The early Christian ideal yields no bright view of this life considered independently of the life to come. It sets no value on any joy in life as life, and holds out no hope of any realizable utopia in the earthly future, such as is forecast by one or two Hebrew prophets. The taint of sin and the shadow of the transitory is everywhere. Life—the winning and the holding of it—runs like a thread of gold throughout the Fourth Gospel. But the context leaves no doubt that the life eternal of the individual soul is always meant, even where this is not explicitly stated. Life eternal is promised to him who "hateth his life in this world." It is true that "the gospel of the kingdom should be preached to all the world," but—"then shall the end come." And this is described in terms of Armageddon. Only in a new heaven and earth should God dwell with men, and with but few who in a former birth had last lived on the old earth. The simile of Noah's little ark and the great flood brooded heavily on the infant Church.

Yet even in the face of this near and

appalling future, appalling as regarded the great majority of mankind, the early Christian estimate of life, as lived by the faithful and holy, that is, taken qualitatively only, was not pessimistic. It was life of a very distinctive quality, like a rare and precious flower in a weedy jungle. It was the result of severe selection. Energy was concentrated. And this kind of life was proved to be so pregnant of joy born of profound conviction and utter devotion, that its greatest votary could bid his followers "Rejoice without ceasing, and again I say unto you, Rejoice!" It is not invariably the hope of the transcendent future that so transformed their estimate of the possibilities of this life. It was largely a condition of heart and mind, the florescence of a new and higher ideal respecting this life, reconciliation with the best they knew, the sense of liberty from lower bonds. "If any man be in Christ, he is a new creature."

Akin to this joy and serenity in a special quality of life is the atmosphere pervading those poems of the Sutta-Pitaka which are ascribed to many of the early Buddhist saints, both men and women. The wonderful awakening that the new life had brought to them: —the realization of the character of the Buddha, of the nature of the Norm, of fraternity with the good, of liberty from harassing bonds, of mental clarity, of having stepped out of and beyond objects in life that used to call up passion, enmity and illusions, the state, that is to say, termed Nibbana (Nirvana) :—all this is hymned as the having put an end for ever to *dukkha*, and the enjoying peace, serenity and rapture.

And the ground for this blissful state had much in common with that of the early Christian. The latter would say that the fact of walking with Christ made this life splendid. The Buddhist *arahant* had carried out his Master's ordinance, and won mental illumination or "freedom." He represented for Buddhism, life raised to its highest value short of Buddhahood itself.

This is what I have meant elsewhere [1] by calling Buddhism optimistic in its qualitatative estimate of life. The Christian saint could humbly admit to moral warfare still rending him at times. The Arahant was believed to have won peace utterly and finally. But with respect to the desirableness of life taken quantitatively, or *en bloc*, Buddhism is, I repeat, frankly pessimistic. The craving for mere life or living was condemned as ignoble, as stupid, as a moral bondage, as one of the four *āsava's*, or (mental) intoxications. The plunge into the full tide of human life, which Faust was to find so "interesting," was, from their point of view, too much compact of Vanity Fair, shambles and cemetery to be worth the plunge. With the faith, however, possessed by all systems of training, in the power of nurture to trans-

[1] *Psychological Ethics*, xciii., lxxxvi.

form, or at least modify nature, it prescribed, for its more serious devotees, a deliberate pruning away of everything which it judged might hinder the evolution of life of a finer, higher quality. These chosen spirits could not afford to cultivate life in breadth and length.

If then, for concrete life, we substitute life of a certain quality, where selective economy concentrates the energies on certain lines of development, Buddhism, so far from depreciating that kind of life, pronounced it fair and lovely to a degree attainable by no mere spell of renewed life spent in celestial regions. It stood for a kind of happiness concerning which the judgment of Western thought has tended to be sceptical: the bliss of attainment, without satiety. Over here we have tried to persuade ourselves that joy lies mainly in pursuing—a pathetic way of reconciling ourselves to failure. This consciousness of final attainment, called by early Buddhism *arahatta* (Araha(n)tship, literally worthiness, fitness), *vimutti* (emancipation, liberty), *aññā* (gnosis, insight), *nibbāna*, is the realization of the final culminating stage in a single stream of life evolving from eternity. The victim of that stream's current has now become the master. The plant—to shift the metaphor—that takes years to reach florescence—has burst into flower, and tastes its "crowded hour of glorious life."

The theory of Arahantship may, or may

not be the effort of an ancient, alien (yet Aryan) culture to interpret natural laws, namely that (1) nature, working through the conscious moral will, as well as through lower organisms, will sacrifice mere quantity of life, if thereby she may gain intensive fulness and more highly evolved quality of life; or (2) that supremely fine development—genius, for instance—tends, not to reproduction, but, having blossomed, to die out. But this anyway is undeniable; if, and in as far as, Buddhism holds this earthly existence capable of producing what it judged to be perfected persons, or saints, it is in a certain way and to a certain degree optimistic, rather than the reverse, in the value it sets on life. A conceivably higher value would have lain in the belief in a future Utopia wherein the majority were Arahants, or nearly so. But Buddhism, like Christianity, is at too close grips with real life for this.

Thus far we have found that the imputation of thorough-going pessimism to the Buddhist ideal is too slovenly for the following reasons:—Movements of religious and ethical reform start necessarily with pessimistic utterances. Buddhism preaches not so much resignation to evil or ill, as revolt and escape from evil or ill. No gospel is wholly pessimistic that sets high value on a certain possible ideal of life.

Indeed it is not unlikely, as Mr. Narasu remarks,[1] that pessimism was, in the first

[1] *Essence of Buddhism*, p. 119.

place, associated with Buddhism through Schopenhauer proclaiming the close agreement between his own teaching and such superficial and ill-based knowledge as he had acquired of Buddhism. The imputation, however, thus somewhat arbitrarily set up, has persisted, and, as we have seen, is liberally renewed at second-hand. It may therefore meet a certain demand, to have examined this particular alleged character of Buddhism. There should certainly be no lack of interestingness in the light such as examination throws, as we have further to see, on the varying standpoints and ideals of humanity.

CHAPTER VII

THE NORM AS IDEAL (*continued*)

THE belief of the Buddhism of the Pitakas in the perfectibility of human individuals on earth—one here, one there, one now and one then—without an eternal immaterial heaven as the indispensable field wherein to attain perfection, is a notable phase in the evolution of human ideas. This consummation was held to be approached by stages of conscious experience entitled the four paths and the four fruits, the fruits being moments of conscious fruition or sense of attainment, forming the culminating point to each path. The paths were termed that of the Stream-attainer, of the Once-Returner (*i.e.* one who was in his penultimate span of life), of the Never-Returner, and of Arahantship. Summarized in terms of spiritual experience, they consisted in a progressive purification of mind and heart from all worldly, other-worldly, sensual, or inimical ideals, and the complete supersession of these by a consciousness of clear insight into the natural evolution of all things, with a background of disinterestedness and benevolence. More of this state of mind in our next chapter.

The undesirable ideals are conceived in such categories as modes of craving, grasping, or unregenerate desire, modes of defilement, corruption or, more literally, torment (*kile'su*), modes of bondage or fetters. The desirable ideal was, as has been stated, conceived positively as Arahantship or topmost path and fruition, and negatively as emancipation and as *nibbāna* (Sanskrit, *nirvāna*).

Around the last-named term, as readers doubtless know, an unparalleled amount of confused ideas has collected. The etymology of the word is as doubtful as is that of our " heaven. Buddhist mediæval text-books are in no doubt about it. " Now, Nibbāna," runs the *Compendium of Philosophy*, " which is reckoned as not concerned with the things of this world (*lok-utt'ără*), is to be realized through the knowledge belonging to the four paths, and is the object of them and of their fruits. It is called Nibbāna, in that it is a de-parture (*ni-vāh*) from that craving which is called *vāna* " (p. 168). But, as this very passage shows, all mediæval etymology, both oriental and occidental, is exegetical. That is to say, the structure of a word is forced into showing, not a primitive meaning, but that which it has come to signify in the tradition followed by the commentator. According to the passage quoted, the word is derived *both* from " away-going " and from no-craving.

This will not pass muster in modern philology. But it is of no great consequence. We have fortunately, in the Pitakas, instances of the older, more literal meaning of the word, showing unmistakably that Nibbāna meant, not going away or forth, but gone out, dying "out" or "extinction," as of an expiring fire.

In the numerous similes and parables of the Buddha's discourses, the kindling and the going out and putting out (*nibbāyati*, *nibbāpeti*) of it are frequently and variously applied. One of these applications is to the three cardinal springs of unregenerate desire, namely, greed, hate and illusion, especially the first. The individual and the world itself are often pictured as being on fire with these, and the regenerate state of one who is in the Four Paths as a process of extinguishing the fires, and the Arahant state as one of extinct fires and "coolness" (*sīti-bhāva*). Here are a few instances: Ānanda the disciple finds another, Vangīsa, conscious of passionate feeling inflaming his thoughts:

> "My sense with passion burns, my mind's aflame !
> O well did Gotama compassionate
> Speak of a putting out (*nibbāpana*). . . ."[1]

In the "Burning" discourse, delivered by the Buddha on Gaya Head,[2] watching it may be—as one may even to-day—a heath fire playing over the slope—the senses and

[1] *Samyutta-Nikāya*, i.　　[2] *Vinaya Texts*, i. 134.

their objects are pictured as burning with lust, enmity and illusion, although the antithetical state to this, namely, Arahantship, is not described as a process of extinct fire.

But in one of the Sisters' shorter poems we get the closest possible association of the ideal with the simple act of extinguishing flame :—

> With ploughshares ploughing up the fields, with seed
> Sown in the breast of earth, men win their crops,
> Enjoy their gains, and nourish wife and child.
> Why cannot I, whose life is pure, who seek
> To do the Master's will, no sluggard am,
> Nor puffèd up, win to Nibbāna's bliss ?
>
> One day, bathing my feet, I sit and watch
> The water as it trickles down the slope.
> Thereby I set my heart in steadfastness,
> As one doth train a horse of noble breed.
> Then going to my cell, I take my lamp,
> And seated on my couch I watch the flame ;
> Grasping the pin, I pull the wick right down
> Into the oil. . . .
> Lo ! the Nibbāna of the little lamp !
> Emancipation dawns ! My heart is free ![1]

There was and is, for Buddhists, a glamour and a thrill in the term Nibbāna, such as we can only feel in the word linked here with it, and which is almost equally negative in form —the term emancipation, freedom or liberty. For them there is no death-knell in the word, but a presentiment of bliss.

[1] *Psalms of the Sisters*, 72. Referred to by Dr. Pischel (*op. cit.*) in this connection.

"There is no fire like unto passion's greed,
No hapless cast of dice like unto hate,
No ill that equals all that makes the self,[1]
Nor is there any bliss greater than peace.
These things to know e'en as they really are,
This is Nibbāna, crown of happiness."[2]

The reference to Nibbāna as supreme happiness in the last line seems to have been a traditional saying in the Buddha's time. Mystery hangs about any religious usage of the term previous to the Pitakas. But in one of the Suttas a verse, similar to that quoted in part above, is referred to as a sort of saw or rune.

The Buddha is represented as conversing with Māgandiya, a recluse, who accuses him of teaching revolutionary doctrines. The Buddha introduces a verse :—

Health is the highest thing to get,[3]
Nibbāna is the highest bliss,
And of all paths the Eightfold 'tis
That unto deathless safety leads.

Māgandiya exclaims: "How strange and wonderful it is, sir, that you should so aptly quote that verse! I have heard my teachers and their teachers also say it." "What then, Māgandiya, is that health, what is that Nibbāna?" Māgandiya strokes his limbs and replies: "Why, this, sir, is health, this is Nibbāna, for I am healthy and well at present, and ail in no respect whatever."

[1] Literally "the Khandhas."
[2] *Dhammapada, vv.* 202, 203.
[3] Cf. *Jātaka,* vol. i. No. 84.

Nothing can show more clearly than this, coupled with the fire-similes, that, when the Pāli books were first compiled, Nibbāna was a word which could mean literally blowing or going out of fire, and yet, at the same time, be symbolical of the cheerful serenity or conscious well-being that accompanies health of mind and body. And nothing is easier, once we cease to "think of something else," *i.e.* the myth that the extinction refers to life, and make it refer to a spiritual and moral disease burning like fire wasting, like fever.[1]

Neither can there be any reasonable doubt but that Buddhism invested the word with a deeper, more spiritual significance. We see it begun, as it were, in the Buddha's further remarks to Māgandiya, while it must not be overlooked that the compilers of the *Samyutta* place the term as a fully accepted name for the goal of the Buddha-doctrine, in the very first sermon :—" By avoiding these two extremes, the Tathāgata has gained knowledge of the middle path which is vision-making, knowledge-making, which makes for calm, for insight, for enlightenment, for Nibbāna."[2] It is in such a string of desirable or ideal states of spiritual attainment that the word is used, in the Sutta-Pitaka more frequently than as an isolated term; for instance: "this is good, this is excellent, to wit, the calming of all karma-activities, the renunciation of all

[1] Rhys Davids, *Early Buddhism* (1908), 73.
[2] *Samyutta-Nikāya*, v. 420 f. ; *Vinaya Texts*, i. 94.

the bases (of rebirth), the destruction of craving, passionlessness, ceasing, nibbāna."[1] Again: "Why has the Exalted One not declared whether the saint (*tathāgata*) exists after death? Because, brother, this is a matter that does not make for things needful to salvation (advantage), nor for that which concerns the holy life, nor for distaste for the world, nor for passionlessness, nor for cessation, nor for calm, nor for insight, nor for enlightenment, nor for Nibbāna." "What then hath the Exalted One declared?" "That which doth make for all these things, to wit: This is Dukkha! This is the cause of Dukkha! This is the cessation of Dukkha! This is the path leading to the cessation of Dukkha!"[2]

But to return to Māgandiya's reply:—The dialogue does not continue, as we doubtless wish it had (and as a later and less genuine document might have done) with a discussion of the term Nibbāna. A higher ideal is substituted. Health and nibbāna are something more than a condition of this poor, faulty, physical frame. Māgandiya is as a blind man, seeking a clean white robe, who is cheated into donning a stained and dirty one. He is advised to join himself to wiser associates (than his wandering recluses), who will teach him the "Ariyan eye"—the

[1] *Anguttara-Nikāya*, ii. 118, and eight parallel passages; *Dīgha-Nikāya*, iii. 130, etc.

[2] *Samyutta-Nikāya*, ii. 223, and many similar passages.

gentle or noble vision—through which he will learn to know health, to see Nibbāna, will learn to put away all craving for the rebirth of body and mind, to give up the clinging to "becoming," and thereby escape the ill-health of *Dukkha*.

If it be asked: "Is there then no more positive definition given of Nibbāna in the Pitakas, the reply is, Certainly; Nibbāna is defined as a synonym for the disciplining (*vin'ăya*) and the destruction (*khăyă*) of *rāga* (passion, lust), *dosa* (hate, anger), and *moha* (illusion, error, dulness), which are called "fires," and again, of the *āsava's* (sensuality, lust for becoming or rebirth, opinion, ignorance). These are answers to the categorical questions: "What is Nibbāna?" "What is a synonym for it?"[1] Elsewhere, with equal terseness, it is stated: "The cessation of becoming is Nibbāna (*bhava-nirodho nibbānam*). This, by the way, is an utterance placed in the mouth of disciples, not of the Master, whose are the preceding statements.[2] Elsewhere, again, Nibbāna is made a synonym for the acquisition or realization of Truth. Here it is the Exalted One who speaks in both passages, which should be mutually compared: (1) "'Tis even as a border town"—the Buddha is illustrating the fact that the roads to truth and

[1] *Samyutta-Nikāya*, iv. 251, 261, 371; v. 8.

[2] *Ibid.*, ii. 115 ff.; *Anguttara-Nikāya*, v. 9, of *Milinda*, i. 106.

insight are not one but many—" having walls and towns and gates, with a wise and prudent gatekeeper keeping out strangers, welcoming friends. From the east comes a pair of messengers, asking for the lord of the city. Him they find at the crossways. And they, delivering a message of truth, depart . . . And other twin messengers come even so from the west, from the north. . . . Now have I made you a parable . . . and this is the meaning. The town is this body; the gates are the senses, the gate-keeper is conscience; the messengers are calm and insight; the lord is mind; the message of truth is Nibbāna. . . ."[1] (2) " This is the supreme Ariyan insight, even knowledge how to destroy all *Dukkha.* This, his liberty, founded on truth, is firm and sure. For that is a lie which is not genuine, and that which is genuine is true, even Nibbāna. . . . For this is the supreme Ariyan truth, even that which is genuine, even Nibbāna."[2]

To this import of moral and intellectual purity, and of the certainty that the end of the long series of living, earthly, heavenly, infernal was at hand, and therewith the end of all suffering, we may add other and favourite Pitaka synonyms for Nibbāna:—*Amătă* the ambrosial, *i.e.*, the immortal, or, more literally, the not-dead; *Acchŭtă*, the not-deceasing; *Acchanta*, the beyond-end; *Akutobhaya*,

[1] *Samyutta-Nikāya*, iv. 195.
[2] *Majjhima-Nikāya*, iii. 245.

the safe, literally, the no-whence-fear; *Anuttara yogakkhema*, the beyond-less security.

Taking all these ideas covered by the word Nibbāna together, we discern that the Buddhist attitude towards the goal of its Dhamma is one that the West has found it easier to call pessimistic than to sympathize withal. The sublimest aspiration is centred on a state of moral and intellectual purity, in this life, with which is bound up the blissful certainty that death, coming in the natural course of things, will, this time, no more be the threshold of new life anywhere in time or space! For the very great number of persons to whom eternal *life* of the soul in a celestial sphere is the only real solution worth entertaining, the Buddhist ideal seems hopeless. It is only natural and even almost necessary for those who see, in the individual life, something begun, spiritually speaking, only when a living soul is breathed into embryo or newborn babe by a creative spirit, and which enters, after only one death, on an eternal career, to claim for this soul extended experiences and opportunities on the other side. But for the Buddhist the individual is now in eternity, has ever been so, and will so continue, when reborn, unless and until he find the way to suspend the causes of rebirth. There is nothing joyless or hopeless about death and after, for all sincerely good Buddhists. Visions, vague and airy, as with us, of long-lived bliss, as well as of rebirth on earth, surround the dying believer, and with these, as with us, are associated faith and hope. The longing for perfection and the rounding off of life's immense pilgrimage comes, at any given moment, to very few, and to them only when, their evolution approaching maturity, a change comes over their ideals, and when the things wherein they, in the past, have, with other men, taken delight, delight them now no more.

Such appears clearly in the old chronicles of Buddhist saints, who have bequeathed us the story of their heart and its quest in the Book of Gāthā's or verses—"psalms" I call them. In these legends it is some good deed, some aspiration, some resolve performed in past ages, which has planted their feet on the long, long, upward road, till at length in the days of "our Buddha" the conditions have matured, and the youth or maiden, man or woman, fulfils her destiny, tastes rapture not of this world, and exults in having done with it all.

There is no uniformity in either the way of their attainment, or in the specific shape which the goal, end, or ideal assumes in each case. I have judged it worth while, in translating this book of the lives and "psalms" of Buddhist saints, to issue a referendum among these single-minded, devoted winners of the *summum bonum* of their faith—some three hundred and thirty-seven in all—inquiring what, in each case, the Nibbāna enjoyed by the Arahant *meant* for him or her. The poems may not always convey all that it meant for each; many of them are too brief for this, and many of them are verses prompted by some particular occasion. Taken together, however, they yield a very instructive number of aspects of attainment, uttered at a time when the movement was beginning to win over the imagination and loyalty of many, and while yet the dew and bloom of youth lay on its ideals.

There is a very large, perhaps the largest consensus of conviction, expressed with more or less rapture, that something has been got rid of: something felt as mainly Ill (*dukkha*) craving (*tanhā*), the triad "greed, hate and illusion," the continuance of Becoming (rebirth or coming back to be), or Bonds of various kinds. More positively expressed, this riddance is pictured, intellectually, as light, insight, truth, gnosis or higher "saving" knowledge; emotionally, as happiness, calm, coolness, content, good, peace, safety; volitionally, as freedom, self-mastery, supreme opportunity, saintly companionship.

It is in this manifold psalm of victory that a fitting comment lies, both to the statement of Dr. Wundt, that the Buddhist ideal is Truth, as the highest fruit of knowledge, and the criticism of Professor Oldenberg,[1] that the early adherents, on the contrary, cared relatively little for knowledge, and were, so

[1] In the *Deutsche Rundschau*, Jan. 1910; translated in the *Buddhist Review*, Oct. 1910.

far as personal devotion to the Buddha did not absorb their thought and feeling, contented rather to await that final dissolution of the long chain of life which should usher in a now inconceivable, but certain Beyond, a being at the back of life, which the attainment of Arahantship, or the firstfruits of Nibbāna, guaranteed to them.

We shall presently consider the relative importance of Truth as an ideal; but we have first briefly to consider this transcendental Nibbāna.

Let us first glance once more at the saints' verses, and, for that matter, to that other probably even older collection, the Sutta-Nipāta, discussed in the essay just mentioned. Sisters and brethren are evidently not looking forward to any state of bliss different from, or higher than that which they are now enjoying. They have won; fruition is theirs; they walk among the sheaves of harvest. Thus one brother:—

> The factors of my life, well understood,
> Stand yet a little while with severed root.
> Sorrow is slain! That quest I've won, and won
> Is purity from fourfold venom's stain.

And a sister:—

> Nibbāna have I realized, and gazed
> Into the mirror of the holy Norm.
> I, even I, am healèd of my hurt.
> Low is my burden laid, my task is done,
> My heart is wholly set at liberty.

And another :—

True happiness is theirs
Who, wise and freed from longing and from doubt,
Cool and serene, have tamed the craving will.

And yet another :—

Now all my sorrows are hewn down, cast out,
Uprooted, brought to utter end,
In that I now can grasp and understand
The base on which my miseries were built.

Craving, the cause, in me is dried up.
Have I not trod, have I not touched the End
Of ill, the Ariyan, the Eightfold Path ?
Oh ! but 'tis long I've wandered down all time,

. . . . . .

Not knowing how and what things really were,
And never finding what I needed sore.
But now mine eyes have seen th' Exalted One ;
And now I know this living frame's the last,
And shattered is th' unending round of births :
No more Pajāpatī shall come to be !

It may be, as I have said elsewhere,[1] that, in thus exulting in their manifold attainment, they implied some state, inconceivable to thought, inexpressible by language, limited as it is to concepts and terms of life as we know it ; a state, neither in time nor in space, yet the sequel of this life's residuum. If so, their common reticence is nothing less than amazing—at least to us, who have not only never been taught, that to crave for transcendental bliss is an error, but have been incited

[1] *Psalms of the Sisters*, xxxi.

to do so. In these verses there is nothing pointing to an unrevealed mystery concerning which "we could an' if we would" sing something. It may be with them as with one who, after long toil and much peril, reaches home, and is content with that for the day, whatever life may yet give or ask for on the morrow. They have won up out of the Maelstrom of the endless round, to something wonderful that now is, but does not call for terms of after-life to describe it; and so resting they sing. So Sister Mittā :—

> Enough for me. I want no heaven of gods!
> Heart's pain, heart's pining have I trained away.

These sentiments, sure only as to the past and present, silent as to the future, might be called the very poetry of Agnosticism, were it not that they are severely concentrated about a certain gnosis, or insight of a positive and not negative nature. Life was judged, by the Buddhist, to be so essentially and inevitably a process of rise and fall, waxing and waning, growth and decay, that to pronounce it, wherever lived, absolutely blissful and eternal, was self-contradiction of the most fundamental kind. In the case of the Arahant, action had become wholly incapable of being transmitted, as cause, to new being, inasmuch as it was no longer the outcome of that form of sensuous desire I have distinguished as craving or thirst (*tanhā*). If then the happy assurance and content hymned in

Arahant utterances of old imply—as, for all we know, they may have implied—a conception of Nibbāna as something involving at final death,

> some sea-change
> Into something rich and strange,

one of two things, at least, is involved : either (*a*) the soul or *attā* was denied not *in toto*, but only as being in any way whatever mixed up with the mind or body (the five khandhas),[1] or (*b*) anyway, life, as we can conceive it, does not exhaust being.

As to the latter assumption—a conception of being, without any of the specific attributes of life—it would not be surprising to encounter a notion of this range in the Indian intellect. To our two-fold logical division of "is," "is not," this intellect reckoned-in two more alternatives : "both is and is not," "neither is nor is not." Hence the Indian reserves the right to conceive, as *logically* possible, that which is neither life nor not-life, neither consciousness nor not-consciousness. Be that as it may, I have come across no such conception as "being, but not life" in Buddhist doctrines ; moreover, if such a notion be implicit in the concept Nibbāna, it is fairly evident that saintly aspiration could scarcely feel, or predicate anything blissful, or otherwise

[1] This heresy is denied at great length in the youngest book of the Abhidhamma-Pitaka, the Kathāvatthu : "Is a personal individuality known as corresponding to fact in any ultimate sense ?"

about it. There could be no enthusiasm about so empty a field of vision. The ancient Christian poet might sing—

> I know not, O I know not
> What joys await us there!

because he could associate joys with *life* eternal in the Blessed City. But the Buddhist, like his pantheistic fellow-countrymen, would have to stop at the first line, matching the *nescio, nescio* with their *neti, neti*, "not thus, not thus." It must suffice that confident expectation be his ineffable bliss. If he gets beyond life, he must drop the terms of life. Of a being not manifested in some kind of person or individual the Buddhist could apparently shape no clearer conception than can we. All speculative writing on Nibbāna so conceived tends to land us in Platonic or other animistic mysticism. We get either an immortality of ideas, as distinct from ideating minds, or we get an abstract absolute Being, from which all the furniture of space and spatialized time have been prescinded, leaving us with, so to speak, the bare concept of pure movement.

The other assumption (*a*) is that of the Sānkhya and Yoga systems. In them, however, unlike Buddhism, the dogma of the individual hyper-phenomenal self is very plainly affirmed. Why should the Buddha have differed from these in confining himself to negative statements about the *attā*, and have drawn down the veil of his "things undeclared"[1] on all questions as to whether there was being for the Arahant, when mental and bodily life was extinct?

A very ingenious answer to this, propounded by Dr. F. Otto Schrader,[2] is that, whereas the Buddha, like the Christ, had many things to say unto his followers which they could not bear then to profit by, he judged it better, for pragmatic reasons, in an age seething with speculative ferment, to make no pronouncement that would inevitably add fuel to such speculations.

An obvious rejoinder to this is that it was equally incumbent on the Buddha, if he was omniscient, to make a positive pronouncement, equally for pragmatic reasons, rather than abandon posterity to an eternity of doubt[3] respecting the final destiny of his saints.

That to which he is recorded, in the Pitakas, to have committed himself, is only this: (1) that at his death the perfected saint became extinct like the flame of an expiring fire, whereof no man could say, the fire gone out went here or went there; (2) that the Annihilationists, who taught destruction at death of the soul, were in error as much as the Eternalists, who taught its continued existence (not because their conclusions were

[1] *Avyākăta*, not-predicated, or unanswered.

[2] *Journal Pāli Text Society*, 1905, "Nirvana."

[3] Cf. *Milinda*, ii. 196, the King's painful perplexity.

wrong, but because they speculated about a mythical object); (3) that all such questions were not conducive to holy living, nor to wisdom, nor to Nibbāna itself. It is also recorded in two of the older collections of discourses, that he used the expression: "perfected with a 'going out' (Nibbāna) wherein is no residuum of life."[1] This expression is used in referring to the death of a Buddha or Arahant only. The word rendered "perfected," *parinibbuta, parinibbāna,* does not mean dying, still less does it mean, as translators often faultily render it, "entered into Nirvāna." Literally, it is "completely gone out," but "gone out" for Buddhists is tantamount to calm and health after purification or training. Hence we find the word applied, by the Buddha, to a horse broken in and docile after fretting and fuming at restraint. Thus also, in the training of human beings, "as no man," runs a Buddha-discourse,[2] "who is himself in a bog can help another out," so will only one who is "himself tamed, disciplined, calmed (*parinibbuto*)," tame, discipline and make calm (*parinibbāpessăti*) another. Nevertheless both noun and verb were technically used by the Buddhists, with or without the reference to "residuum of life," for the final death of a perfected human being, in contradistinction

[1] *Anguttara-Nikāya,* ii. 120; iv. 202, 313; *Dīgha-Nikāya,* iii. 135.

[2] *Majjhima-Nikāya,* i. 446; 45.

to the other technical term for the death of a being not yet perfected, namely "he did time (*kālam akāsi*)."

The terms [*sa-*]*upādisesa*, *anupādisesa*, meaning with, and without residual vital conditions, or bases of life, respectively, occur at rare intervals, either singly, or together in the Sutta-Pitaka. Buddhaghosa paraphrases the pair by "with, and without remainder of *upādāna*"—a word signifying both "grasping" and "fuel," and thus denoting, both subjectively and objectively, the cause of renewed living (see p. 91). His exegesis may not be etymologically sound, but it is none the worse Buddhism for that. The terms are applied to a saintly career which is in either the penultimate or the final span of life. Of early post-canonical works the *Netti-pakărăna* uses the pair without commenting on them, but the *Milinda*, the dialogues in which on Nibbāna are instructive and very beautiful, does not use either of the terms. The mediæval digest *Compendium of Philosophy*, merely mentions the two terms as convenient verbal, or logical, but not actual, distinctions in a notion:—Nibbāna—which is really, as it states, "in its nature single" (p. 168).

This pair of terms, however, although thus divested of deep-cleaving significance, has been laid hold of by the incorrigible speculative tendency of man in East as in West, starved by the reserve of the founders of

Buddhism. Other passages moreover have been adduced, from sayings ascribed to the Buddha, which to some thinkers are satisfying evidence that, in the case of perfected human beings, who in this life attain Nibbāna, final death was not, by that teacher, considered as the be-all and end-all of life's long cycle. To Vaccha, the Brahmin, for instance, he declares that whatever material form or mental constituent be declared as composing such a being, "all this he has put away, cut off, made like the stump of a palm-tree, made non-existent, and unable to arise in the future. Now he, thus set free from all the khandhas, is deep, immeasurable, hard to fathom, even as is the ocean. Hence it does not fit the case to say: 'he is reborn,' 'he is not reborn,' or both, or neither."

Judging by other contexts, this state of a Tathāgata (which may be rendered Buddha, or perhaps Arahant also) does not describe him at death only, but is his potential condition during his lifetime. The Buddha, anyway, declares that Vaccha's training and tradition make it very hard for him to see and to follow.[1] But here are other passages deemed crucial:—A disciple asks the Master:

> For souls in mid-stream standing, aye oppressed
> By age and death in fearsome rising flood,
> Tell thou me of an island, Master, tell!

[1] *Majjhima-Nikāya*, i. 486-8.

The Buddha answers:

Nothing, naught-holding, such that matchless isle.
Nibbāna—such the name I tell to thee.
'Tis the destruction of old age and death.

And elsewhere in the same collection:

. . . the saint, when released from mind and body,
Flits into oblivion, is accounted for no longer.

Hath he but flitted? Or is he then no longer?
Or doth he live to eternity made whole?

Nowhere is measure for one gone to oblivion,
That whereby we speak of him—that exists no longer.
Wholly cut off are all forms of our knowing,
Cut off the channels of speech, every one.[1]

These two groups of quotations, taken together with the pair of terms distinguishing two phases in Nibbāna, are held by some thinkers[2] to justify the view that Nibbāna referred not only to assurance of present salvation, but also to an after-state neither mental nor bodily, neither in time nor in space, "inaccessible to the forms of thought which hold good on earth," wherein is no individuality nor shadow of a person. Western views on the subject are easily accessible. I will rather quote from the letter of a European Pāli scholar, in Burma, Mr. Duroiselle, reporting on the state of speculative opinion there:—

"The great mass of the people, whose

[1] *Sutta-Nipāta*, 1091-3, 1074-5.
[2] *Cf.* Prof. Oldenberg, *e.g.*, *op. cit.*

Buddhism is deeply tinged with Shamanism, believe in a life to come after the Arhat's death. The learned Bhikkhus, on the other hand, may be grouped, in this connexion, into three divisions :—(1) Nirvana is complete extinction. This can be proved from the Pitakas. (2) Nirvana is a glorious life (!) of eternal happiness. This can be proved from the Pitakas. (3) Nirvana is the mystery of Buddhism, and no one knows what it really is. The Buddha never made any definite statement about it. This can be proved from the Pitakas. Class 3 is the most numerous, but *tends* to agree with 1."

I quote my correspondent's letter with all possible editorial reserve. The state of opinion would doubtless have been differently worded by a Buddhist, whether this report agreed in substance or not. In this little work, however, we are less concerned to discuss discussion, than to inquire into original doctrines and their evolution along a certain line of tradition. And the result of our inquiry is firstly, an original ideal or goal of life, conceived to be realizable only by a mental and moral training, which sapped at the very springs of all revival of life after death. (2) A refusal either to predicate anything concerning a prolongation of perfected being, along, possibly, with a refusal to find any such state about which to predicate. (3) A tradition which leaves its followers divided, and unorthodoxly speculative, on this very point, but *not therefore in the least disposed* either to find their creed pessimistic, or to waver in their faith. For all other creeds, doubt and perplexity on such a matter would be productive of both these results, and therefore fatal. Their followers will tend to judge Buddhism amiss, simply because they are "thinking of something else." For this one creed, its great perspective of present eternal life and rebirth, and of a cyclical evolution towards maturity of a self-transforming identity, relegates this question of the nature and destiny of saintship to its remote and serene mountain-summit. Arahantship is as rare for them as is saintship among ourselves. For the mass of good average folk, going, with the patience and courage of all sane mortals, through stage after stage of green immaturity, through the joys and sorrows that have recurred, and will recur so infinitely often, heaven and purgatory and earth itself await their future. Thus much of prospect suffices.

For those who, with the call of the goal supreme sounding in their hearts, have drunk deep of the ancient gospel of Ill and the Ending of Ill, preached in the strife and ardour of religious revival, and who feel, it may be, the malaise of maturing conditions and of the fulness of time pressing upon them, —is it not possible for us, in their case, so to dissever that goal supreme from all connexion with expansion of individual being, that we may read in the Buddha's silence an endorsement of this modern judgment :—" Reason mercifully interposes an impenetrable veil between us and any reality which is wholly alien to our nature" ?

CHAPTER VIII

THE QUEST OF THE IDEAL

OUR educational curricula are designed to meet the needs of all classes of circumstances and intelligence. And we do not expect to find more than a very small minority capable or desirous of availing itself of such instruction and such tests as it has taken the most highly trained intellect of the day to provide. Nor do we hold it unfair that the great majority is not able to benefit directly by the heavy outlay that goes to the output of a few. Similarly there is much doctrine in the Pāli Suttas which was never intended as food for householders and their families, but which, like the standards set up in Christ's Sermon on the Mount, held out objects and prospects unattractive save to the few who, in the words of one chronicler, were being driven by the impending maturity of their spiritual evolution. The distinction here drawn is not between the Order and the laity, for many of the former were not more single-minded in leaving the world than is the case with religious brethren generally. In their case many, especially in India, were called, but few were chosen. Moreover cases are given of laymen and laywomen advancing far in the Paths, full of devotion and intelligence. Of the laity in general, not to speak of discourses and conversations to and with individuals, the whole duty, as conceived by early Buddhism, may be said to be laid down in the Sigalovāda Suttanta, or the lesson given to Sigāla, a pious young layman.[1]

But the limits of this volume leave but a little space to add a few notes on the training and tests of the more interesting minority. These notes may be based on a brief summary of the Threefold Training, occurring in the Sutta-Pitaka, under which, in the Order, the life and exercises judged fittest to carry the student right up to the goal were grouped.

"There are three grades of training, bhikkhus; which are the three? The higher ethics (*sīla*, literally, habit; *cf.* the Greek, *ēthos*), the higher consciousness, the higher insight (or wisdom). What is the higher ethics? When a Bhikkhu lives by the code of discipline, and in conformity to the precepts of morality; when he sees danger in small offences; when having undertaken the precepts he practises them."

"What is the second grade? When a Bhikkhu, aloof from sense-appetites, aloof from evil thoughts, enters into and abides in the First Jhāna (rapt meditation), wherein attention

[1] *Or Singāla. Dīgha-Nikāya,* iii. 180. A translation is reprinted in the *Buddhist Review,* Jan. 1911.

is directed and sustained, which is born of solitude and filled with zest and pleasurable emotion; when, next, from the subsiding of attention, initial and sustained, he enters into and abides in the Second Jhāna, which is inward tranquillizing of the mind, self-contained and uplifted from the working of attention; which is born of concentration, full of zest and pleasurable emotion; when, next, through the quenching of zest, he abides indifferent, and enters and abides in the Third Jhāna, mindful and fully conscious, experiencing in the body that pleasure whereof the Ariyans declare 'He who is indifferent but mindful dwells in happiness.' When, next, by putting away both pleasant and painful emotion, by the dying out of the joy and misery he used to know, he enters into and abides in the Fourth Jhāna, that utterly pure mindfulness and indifference, wherein is neither happiness nor unhappiness."

"What is the third grade? When a Bhikkhu knows as it really is that 'This is Ill; this is the cause of Ill; this is the cessation of Ill; this is the way leading to the cessation of Ill.'"

An alternative reply to the last question is then added: "When a Bhikkhu, by exterpating the intoxicants (the four *āsava's*), has of himself comprehended and realized, even in this life, sane (*an-āsava*) emancipation of heart and of insight."

Then follow these verses:—

Whoso hath zeal, courage and energy,
Is apt to meditate, alert of mind,
Guarding the forces of his body well,
Let him pursue the threefold higher walk,
Loftiest code of conduct, mind, insight,
From first to last, the last even as the first,
Above, below, by night e'en as by day.
Hath he thus every quarter [of his life]
Mastered with infinite concentration rapt,
This do they call the training and the course
And eke the pure and holy pilgrimage.
Him do they call The Wakened of the World,
Brave hero faring to the Way's high End.
To him when consciousness doth near its end,
To him from craving utterly set free,
NIBBANA of the burning flame[1] hath come,
And to his heart Release and Liberty.[2]

Under the first head we see comprised a discipline for the conduct both of the body and the social self (to use William James's expression); under the second, we have a scheme for taming and training the mind, considered as an instrument beating out its reactions, cognitive, emotional, volitional. Under the third we have this trained mind confronting the most general or philosophical problems of life.

Concerning the attitude of the man-or-woman-in-orders toward the body, the Buddha in the address to a few former fellow-ascetics with which he inaugurated his career as a teacher, advocated a "middle path," opposed

[1] "As it were of a lamp," runs Buddhaghosa's Commentary.

[2] *Anguttara-Nikāya*, i. 236 f.

equally to self-indulgence and to self-mortification. There was obvious logic in such a position, springing from his view, set out in a preceding chapter, of *Dukkha.* The former course led sooner or later to pain and sorrow; the latter was painful from the first.

India has perhaps elaborated the gospel of salvation through asceticism further than any other country. Such practices were held to benefit not only the ascetic, but the lay-world who, so to speak, "ran" him and won merit by his presence. Such practices were spoken of collectively as *tăpăs,* "burning" or "glow," and they constituted a system parallel to, but mostly independent of, any contemporary system of salvation by sacrificial rites. They are all condemned, no less than such rites, by the Sutta-Pitaka as different forms of tormenting either the self, or others, namely animals and slaves.

There was only one kind of "burning" cultivated by Buddhism. This was the "ardent" (*ātāpin*) disposition of the earnest soul, whose sensitive conscience would feel, not, as we say, the bite of re-*morse*, but those burning (*tapaniya*) states when realizing: "I have left undone those things that I ought to have done, and done those things that I ought not to have done."[1] It was only those who had got beyond all this, who could be described as "become cool."

In theory, religiously considered, the body

[1] *Anguttara-Nikāya,* i. 49.

was, for Buddhists, as for Christians who had left the world, a "foul" or "vile" thing, and the senses so many channels of danger and suffering. Susceptibility to beauty of person needed correction by episodes in training involving the contemplation of decaying objects. The more practical aspect of physical culture was to care so far for the needs of the body, as to press it into the service of the quest for Arahantship. To this conclusion the Buddha came, as he is made to relate, after severe *tapas* had almost worn the life out of him: "Not by this bitter course of painful hardship shall I arrive at that separate and supreme vision of all-sufficing Ariyan knowledge, passing human ken. Might there not be another path to enlightenment?"[1] And he forthwith took nourishment, and for the meditations that brought enlightenment, chose a fair woodland spot soothing and bracing to sense. From that time austerities troubled him no more. A recluse compliments him on the way his disciples honoured him for his frugal, simple life and love of solitude. "That can hardly be," he replies, "for while some of my disciples affect ascetic practices, I some days eat more, or wear robes made for laymen, or accept invitations to dine, or dwell indoors, or among my fellows."[2] And in the rules of the Order the body is to be decently draped, cleansed and massaged, regularly fed, sheltered in the

[1] *Majjhima-Nikāya*, i. 246. [2] *Majjhima-Nikāya*, ii. 5 f.

rainy season, rested during the noonday heat, and medically heated when ailing. For prolonged meditation the posture of sitting upright with crossed legs was chosen as, for Oriental habits, freest from discomfort. The ascetic practices alluded to persisted and came later to be grouped as a scheme of thirteen extra vows or burdens.[1] But the spirit of early Buddhism was to reduce living to a healthful simplicity, at least for those who had devoted their lives to realizing the ideal, and to propagate the Norm. So they would get near to the liberty of the bird—to use the Buddhist metaphor—which in flying " bears with it but the power to fly."

The monachistic habit or practice of seclusion in the wild, common to Indian recluseship from time immemorial, and probably imported from India to Egypt and so to the newly Christianized Europe, was largely and systematically practised by Buddhists. It was both practised by the founder himself,[2] and recommended to the follower, as the best opportunity for cultivating detachment, spiritual calm, and thorough-going meditation on any given subject prescribed by the recluse's superior. Many of the Order, unfitted for taking part, even as teachers, in the battle of life, spent all their days in seclusion, being known as forester Bhikkhus. Others sought the silence of the upland woods and caves to complete the utter mastery of detachment,

[1] *Milinda*, ii., Bk. VI. [2] *Vinaya Texts*, ii. 312 f.

requisite to usher in the cool and peace of Nibbāna, or to recruit from wearing mission work.

The poems of the saints to which I have referred afford an interesting pageant of glimpses into the ways of these lonely commoners of air. And it is pleasant to see how largely the joy of life in the wild (generally supposed to be a phase of modern consciousness only) gets blended with the spiritual aspirations. We see the solitary as a lover of the heights—were they not "clean and pure," "lonely and free from crowds," "a hiding-place," and type of the lofty thoughts of great minds? [1] We see him "become in heart a wild creature," filled with the "forest sense of things" (*araññasaññī*), bathing in mountain tarn, listening in his cave to the music of the rains and to the crash of the storm, joying in the beauty of crag and cloud, of verdure and blossom, of bird-life and the cries of forest-creatures.

I am tempted just here to stray off the high road of our subject, and invite the reader for a few moments to follow these men and women to whom I have lent Burns' fine phrase, and sample this early Wordsworthian note in their poems. The discovery of it was a keen delight, and there is no point in early Buddhism less hackneyed; for although Professor Oldenberg's scholarly edition of the Brethren's

[1] *Milinda*, ii. 353: "On the alpine qualities of a bhikkhu."

poems (the late Professor Pischel's fit pendant of the Sisters' poems included) was one of the first publications of the Pali Text Society (1883), the attention of English readers, so far as I know, was never drawn to it till two years ago.[1]

Of the 264 poems ascribed to these early Arahants, about one-sixth treat of the environing nature and its charm, either by an incidental touch, or in considerable detail. In most instances, seclusion in wild nature is made the background for higher themes. In some cases, the joy of life in the wild is blended and made co-equal with the spiritual theme. In a few poems the theme is Nature pure and simple.

Calling these three groups, A, B, and C, I give examples of each :—

A.

VIMĂLĂ

(in his hill-cave in Kosala, after a thunderstorm).

The burdened earth is sprinkled by the rain,
The winds blow cool, the lightnings roam on high.
Eased and allayed th'obsessions of the mind,
And in my heart the spirit's mastery.

ANGULIMĀLA.[2]

. . . Deep in the wild beneath some forest tree,
Or in the mountain cave, now here, now there,

---

[1] In my article, "The love of nature in Buddhist poems," in the *Quest*, April, 1910.

[2] See p. 162.

I stand and let my over-chargèd heart
Transported beat. Happy I seek my rest,
Happy I rise, happy I pass the day,
Remote from evil—ah! how shall I tell
The sweet compassion of my Lord for me!

B.

EKAVIHARIYA

(Lone-dweller).

To him for whom there's nothing left—before
Or after, or elsewhere—exceeding good
It is that he do live in woods alone.
Lo! now alone I'll get me hence and go
To lead the forest-life the Buddha praised,
In quest of happiness and still retreat.
Yea, swiftly and alone and for my good
I'll seek the jungle that I love, the haunt
Of elephants, th'ascetic's realm of joy,
Where, in Cool-Wood's green shade cool waters lie
Within the mountain glen: there will I bathe
My limbs, and to and fro I'll roam alone.

Lone and unmated in the lovely woods,
When shall I come to rest, work wrought, heart
    cleansed?
Oh! that I might win through who am so fain!
I only may achieve the task; herein
None other may accomplish aught for me.
I'll bind my spirit's armour on, and so
The jungle will I enter, that I'll not
Come forth again until Nibbana's won.
I'll seat me on the mountain-top, the while
The wind blows cool and fragrant on my brow,
And burst the baffling mists of ignorance.
Then on the flower-carpet of the wood,
Anon in the cool cavern of the cliff,
Bless'd in the bliss of Liberty I'll take

Mine ease in thee, old Fastness o' the Crag.[1]
My heart's desire fulfilled, e'en as the moon
On fifteenth day,—all deadly canker slain,
And never more Sa*m*sāra's round for me!

BHŪTA.

When in the lowering sky thunders the stormcloud's drum,
And all the pathways of the birds are thick with rain,
The brother sits within the hollow of the hills
Alone, rapt in thought's ecstasy—no higher bliss
Is given to men than this.

Or where by rivers on whose bank together crowd
Full many a flower, and fragrant rushes scent the air,
With heart serene the brother sits upon the strand
Alone, rapt in thought's ecstasy—no higher bliss
Is given to men than this. . . .

C.

SAPPĀKA.

Whene'er I see the crane, her clear, pale wings
Outstretched in fear to flee the black storm-cloud,
A shelter seeking, to safe shelter borne,
Then doth the river Ajakara*n*ī
Give joy to me.
Whene'er I see the crane, her plumage pale
And silver-grey outstretched in fear to flee
The black storm-cloud, seeing no refuge nigh,
The refuge seeking of the rocky cave,
Then doth the river Ajakara*n*ī
Give joy to me.
Who doth not love to see on either bank
Clustered rose-apple trees in fair array,
Beyond the great cave of the hermitage,

---

[1] Girib'bājā, the ancient burg near the new Rājagaha of the Buddha's time.

Or hear the soft croak of the frogs, their foes
The winged myrmidons withdrawn, proclaim;
Not from the mountain streams is't time to-day
To flit. Safe is the Ajakaranī.
She brings us luck. Here is it good to be!

KASSAPA THE GREAT.[1]

* * * * *

Towering like battlements of azure cloud,
Like pinnacles on lofty castle built,
Re-echoing to the cries of jungle folk:
Those are the highlands of my heart's desire.
Fair uplands rain-refreshed and resonant
With crested creatures' cries antiphonal,
Where venerable Rishis oft resort;
Those are the highlands of my heart's desire.
Here is enough for me who fain would dwell
In meditation rapt and solitude.
Here is enough for me who fain would seek
Well-being undisturbed in calm retreat.

* * * * *

The Commentary on these poems, compiled by Dhammapāla in or just before the sixth century A.D. from earlier records (so he says), now lost, gives a brief account of the life of each Brother, and of the circumstances leading up to the poem. MSS. of this work are very rare, and until we were able to purchase one from Burma, there was but one in Europe, at Copenhagen, and that unfinished. The former MS. is now in process of being edited,[2] and, in the case of Brethren like the

[1] Leader of the Order after the Buddha had passed away. The stanzas above are but a sample of the whole.

[2] By Miss Mabel Hunt.

foregoing, its contents throw their genuine feeling for nature into clearer relief. Thus in one Thera's story we read: "And because he loved the woods, he was known as Woodland-Vaccha. . . . And it was in praise of the forest life that he uttered his poem, replying to the bhikkhus who asked him:

"'What comfort can you find in the forest?'

"'Jewels, my friends, from forest and from mountain'":—

> Crags with the hue of heaven's blue clouds,
> Where lies embosomed many a shining tarn
> Of crystal-clear cool waters. . . .

Again, of Usabha it is written: "Finishing his novitiate, he went to study in the forests of Kosala at the foot of the mountains. Now at the time of the rains, the clouds had emptied themselves on the crests of the hills, and trees, bushes and creepers waxed dense with foliage. Then the Thera, going forth one day from his cave, saw the loveliness of the woods and the mountains and considered seriously: "These trees and creepers are unconscious, yet by the season's fulfilment have they won growth. Why should not I, who have also obtained a suitable season, win growth in the things that are good?" And he uttered this verse:—

> The trees on high, by towering clouds refreshed
> With the new rain, break forth in verdant growth.
> To Usabha, who for detachment longs,
> And hath the forest sense of things, doth come
> From this responsive time abundant good.

We are irresistibly reminded here of that modern autumn pendant, in which, with a diametrically opposite philosophical basis and religious faith, the nature-lesson and the spiritual response are yet so parallel :—

> Yet wait awhile and see the calm leaves float
> Each to his rest beneath their parent shade.
>
> * * * *
>
> Unconscious they in waste oblivion lie . . .
> Man's portion is to die and rise again.
> Yet he complains. . . .[1]

The Sisters' poems show an absence of this nature-love that is in them only natural. They are more occupied with the fact of their new freedom of mobility. For them, solitude in the woods, in springtime hours especially, was a new and fearful joy, liable to be marred by male intruders and the call of sense and sex.

> Young art thou, Sister, and faultless—what seekest *thou* in the holy life ?
> Cast off that yellow-hued raiment and come ! . . .

But they, too, were feeling after wider and higher standpoints, which might be forwarded through communing with their ancient and forgotten Mother. There are one or two among their poems, naïf and stammering compared with their brethren's more fluent lyrics, which have for me the deeper pathos of

[1] Keble's " Red o'er the forest peers the setting sun."—*Christian Year.*

[2] *Psalms of the Early Buddhists*, i. 150.

the halting notes of a bird, when first let out into the woods from a cage :

> Though I be suffering and weak, and all
> My youthful spring be gone, yet have I come
> Leaning upon my staff, and clomb aloft
> On mountain peak. My cloak have I thrown off,
> My little bowl o'erturned : so sit I here
> Upon the rock. And o'er my spirit sweeps
> The breath of Liberty ! I win, I win
> The Triple Lore ! The Buddha's will is done ![1]

Turning to the second group of disciplines, I must pass perforce with the barest comment over the ancient fourfold Jhāna formula. The practice was not specifically Buddhistic. " In India from the soma frenzy in the Vedas, through the mystic reveries of the Upanishads, and the hypnotic trances of the ancient Yoga, allied beliefs and practices had never lost their importance and their charm.[2] But the whole subject still awaits competent treatment. Jhāna meditation was the reverse of desultory reverie, and was to be entered upon, after much practice, by closing the avenues of sense through a hypnotic exhaustion of the sense of sight. Now, amongst ourselves knowledge of hypnosis is in its infancy. We are not prepared to admit that a greater freedom and clarity of imagination, representative and constructive, may be secured by blocking out sense-impressions

[1] *Psalms of the Early Buddhists*, i., 28. On the love of nature in the Brethren's poems, see my article in *The Quest*, April, 1910.

[2] Rhys Davids' *Early Buddhism*, 86.

artificially. But this is what Buddhists claim for the practice, as systematized by them. Complete trance might indeed be induced, but not by the four first stages quoted above. The object of these four was to render emotion and intellect tamed, plastic and harmonious. The more ulterior objects were (1) for one who was not aiming directly at Arahantship, to produce a tendency to rebirth hereafter in one of the sublimer, *i.e.*, more dematerialized heavens; (2) for one aiming at Arahantship here and now, to produce a tendency to the Nibbāna-consciousness, by suppressing certain states and dispositions pictured as five "hindrances" and ten "fetters." These were sensual, malevolent, slothful and doubting moods, a hankering after precisely the heavens aspired to by others, conceit or egoism, distraction or excitement, and lastly ignorance.[1] Incidentally, attainment in Jhāna was held to induce a peculiar bliss, and is still held, in Buddhist countries, where it is practised by a small minority, to have this power.[2]

The reader, with his own ancient tradition strong in him, may judge that, if all mental states be brought, through Jhāna, under control, this can only mean that a controller must be functioning, whether we call it ego,

[1] *Psychological Ethics*, lxxxvii.-xc.; *Samyutta-Nikāya*, v. 308, 309.

[2] S. Z. Aung, *Compendium*, 57. E. R. Rost, "Meditation," *Buddhist Review*, Oct. 1911.

soul or spirit. Perhaps this thought tended to intrude itself also among those who practised Jhāna. Such a view was judged, as we have seen, to be illusory (like our "sun-rising" myth), and the danger of it lends significance to the listing of conceit (*māna*) about the ego to the fetters just mentioned. The great innovation made by the Buddha in the philosophy of the ego calls at this point for some digressive discussion. There is to superficial consideration something contradictory in a theory which swept aside the "I" as absolute, as super-phenomenal, and yet which was accompanied by a practical discipline of such self-concentrated regard. Nevertheless, the discipline was prescribed chiefly that the theory might be the better understood.

It was precisely through the plurality and manifoldness of our experience, conceived as pictures, etc., passing before a static, unchanging beholder, that the more crudely conceived "inner man" evolved into the abstract self or ego. The stages of Jhāna were intended to break up this perspective deemed illusory. First, the attention by way of sense-cognition is hypnotically stimulated and concentrated, till mind working through sense is arrested. Then intellectual zest or keen interest dies away; and then mind as happy, easeful emotion ceases, and a sort of zero-point is attained, leaving the vaguer consciousness of wide abstraction:—infinity of space; next, infinity of receptive consciousness (*viññāna*), a potentiality of sensation and emotion, but with no actuality; then as it were a negative consciousness, or awareness that the preceding stage, so far from revealing any persisting entity, was " nothing whatever " (*n'atthi kiñci*). Finally, a stage is reached described as neither conscious nor unconscious, faint and delicate mentality fading into complete trance. And the expert Jhānist could so predetermine this self-hypnosis as to induce it and emerge from it when he chose.[1] But beside its use as a discipline of the will, or voluntary intellection, the philosophic inference he was taught to infer from it was, that after every abstractable phase had been prescinded from consciousness, no abstract Self revealed itself " at the back of " mind.

" Serene, pure, radiant is your person, Sāriputta; where have you been to-day ? " asks one great apostle of another. " I have been alone, in first Jhāna, brother," is the reply, " and to me came never the thought: *I* am attaining it; *I* have emerged from it. And thus, is the comment, individualizing and egoistical tendencies have been well ejected for a long while from Sāriputta ! "[2] And so on, through the four grades, and other five grades of undifferentiated imagining till trance had been reached.

This unobtrusion of the self attained the

[1] *Majjhima-Nikāya*, Suttas 43, 44.

[2] *Samyutta-Nikāya*, iii. 235.

Founder's explicit approval in a more general connexion than the practice of Jhāna. As with some phases of evangelical Christianity, so with Buddhism was it customary for one attaining to the consciousness of Nibbana to testify solemnly to the same. Two disciples thus attaining are related to have waited on the Buddha, and to have thus made confession of their faith: "Lord, he who is Arahant, who has destroyed the intoxicants (*āsavas* of illusion), who has lived the life, who has done that which was to be done, has laid aside the burden, has won his own salvation, has utterly destroyed the fetters of becoming, is by perfect knowledge emancipated,[1] to him it does not occur: "There is who is better than *I*, equal to *me*, inferior to *me*." So saying, they made obeisance and went out. And the Master said, "Even so do men of true breed declare the gnosis they have won; they tell of their gain (*attha*), but they do not bring in the ego (*attā*)."[2]

Once more, we find the Buddha, when the self had been obtruded, diverting the point of the episode to the duty of altruistic regard. The story is told, in the Udāna, a little manual of short episodes framing a metrical *logion*, that the king of Kosala and his wife discuss the Ātmanistic or Vedântist doctrine that the Self (the immanent deity) is dearer

[1] These are all standard formulas, attesting saintship.

[2] *Anguttara-N.*, iii. 359.

than all else.[1] It may be that to the royal pair the idea conveyed no more and no less than to a Christian do the words, "What shall a man give in exchange for his soul?" Any way the king mentions the conversation to the Buddha, who thereupon replies:

> The whole wide world we traverse with our thought,
> Nor come on aught more dear to each than Self.
> Since aye so dear the Self to other men,
> Let the Self-lover harm no other man!

To resume:—for the Buddhist of the Pitakas danger lurked in every form of sustained self-reference, whether the reference arose from metaphysical, psychological, ethical or eschatological considerations. All such emphasis in the mind was classed as *māna*, a word which much resembles in meaning our composite term "conceit," and which we find thus connected: "mind involved in 'I'-making, 'mine'-making conceit."[2] Because Buddhism in India, as it succumbed to Vedântism, became associated with the metaphysic of appearance and reality, it is supposed to be much concerned with *māyā*, or illusion (*i.e.*, of phenomena as unreal). But for early, and all subsequent Theravāda Buddhism, *mānā*, and not *māyā*, is the only world of illusion that is considered, and that really matters. The context of the quotation just given is the problem of practical philo-

[1] *Brihadāranyaka Upanishad*, 1, 4, 8.
[2] *Samy.-Nik.*, ii. 253; iii. 80.

sophy and religion : how—given the recipient organism and the world of external impressions—to attain spiritual freedom, and not to suffer the conceit of self-reference to arise.

There are other formulated methods for regulating mental procedure beside the Jhāna practice. They are called wisdom-winged states of mind, or the name may be also rendered things pertaining to enlightenment. They aim more at training will and intellect. Jhāna is more concerned with control of sense and emotion, in order the better to think. They include the famous category called the Ariyan or Noble Eightfold Path, which, in the earliest teaching, is put forward as in itself a sufficient guide and means to Arahantship, or, as the last of the four Ariyan or Noble Truths, as the way for putting an end to Dukkha. Simple code of ethics as it seems at first sight to be, the qualifying word *sammā* (=*summa*, supreme) attached to each factor denoted the high ideal to be aimed at, and the severe standard to judge by.

Another discipline for the systematic expansion and control of ethical emotion was that known as the Sublime Moods, or the Illimitables. Here the sentiments of love, pity and sympathizing joy were to be taken severally and, commencing with known individuals, be made to suffuse or pervade first these, then groups, ever widening till the whole world of sentient things was included. The fourth sentiment, equanimity, cultivated similarly, would serve to compose and regulate the preceding sentiments. Akin to these was the elemental disposition; fire-heart, water-heart, etc. wherein the consideration of the earth, *e.g.*, patiently suffering things clean or unclean cast upon it, was to abate all feelings of resentment—an association resembling Christ's illustration of the impartial sun.

Absence of resentment—and of the expression of resentment—is a practice that would of itself go far to abolish *dukkha*. However, let it not be supposed that the more positive effort in ethical emotion enjoined above lacked comprehensive statement. One of the better known Pitakan expressions of universal benevolence is, as such, unsurpassed in ancient literature.

> E'en as a mother watcheth o'er her child,
> Her only child, as long as life doth last,
> So let us, for all creatures, great or small,
> Develop such a boundless heart and mind.
> Ay, let us practise love for all the world,
> Upward and downward, yonder, thence,
> Uncramped, free from ill-will and enmity.[1]

This figure of the mother and her child, Buddhaghosa connects with the foregoing Sublime Moods in a pretty passage of exegetics. Namely, her desire for her child's growth is as the first of the four (*mettā*), for her child's recovery from sickness, as the second (*karunā*), for the maintenance of the

[1] *Sutta-Nipātā*, verses 149, 150; *Khuddăka-pātha*, ix.

talents he shows promise of, as the third (*muditā*), while her care not to hinder the career of her grown-up son is as the fourth (*upekkhā*).

In this chapter we are dealing not with the active life of Brother or Sister in early Buddhism, but with the training. It is to be hoped, therefore, that, in all fairness to this practical side of the Dhamma, it will not be supposed that, for a member of the Order, "sublime" sentiments were held to constitute in themselves the ethical life. And yet this is what a distinguished pioneer writer on Buddhism—the late Spence Hardy—with a foreigner's characteristic want of *muditā*, could bring himself to say,[1] namely, that the bhikkhu thought about the virtues of solidarity without practising them. These exercises were but preparations of heart and will for that ministering to the, mainly, spiritual and intellectual needs of others, to which life in the Order was largely devoted, and the importance of which our zeal for material forms of generosity and ministration scarcely appreciates at its real value, so sorely are "the poor ever with us." And Buddhism did not believe in giving free rein to good impulses unregulated by intellectual control.

But no encouragement was permitted to emotional expansion except in intimate dependence upon the culture of ideas and the will. And for the Buddhist, not to say the

[1] *Eastern Monachism*, 249.

Indian, thought and will were, even logically, hardly distinguishable. *Che'tănā*, which modern Buddhists identify with volition, is, etymologically, only "thinking," *chitta* and *cheto* being consciousness, thought, or "heart" in the meaning it had for us in our Jacobean Bible.[1] And all intellection has *chet'anā* as its principal factor. This intimate connection between thinking and willing is further revealed in the disciplines for developing abnormal psychic faculty, known as *iddhi*, a subject into which we cannot now go. Our psychology, till recent years, has been highly developed on the subject of sense-cognition, and for us intellect is mainly receptive and co-ordinating and ratiocinative. But the Indian mind has ever held that thought can translate itself into outgoing energy, not only by way of the voice and the limbs For the Buddhist, man did not indeed make gods in his own image, but he had latent within him god-like and creative powers, such as severe training might develop.

Where we best see emotion pressed by Buddhism into the service of thought and

[1] *E.g.*, "Why reason ye in your hearts?" . . . "Out of the heart proceed evil thoughts," etc. It is for the student of Buddhist philosophy a matter of great interest to note, that one of the most constructive intellects among philosophical reformers has just published an essay in which, all unwittingly, the Buddhist *conclusion* is worked up to by the light of modern knowledge.—*Journal of Psychology*, Dec., 1911: S. Alexander, "Foundations and Sketch-plan of a Conational Psychology."

will, is in its attitude towards Desire. The whole world of earth, with its purgatories[1] and its nearer heavens, is conceived and named in terms of desire, that is *kāma*, desire being understood very generally, as wishing or wanting. And that which wishes or wants, is known as *tanhā* (Sanskrit *trishnā*), always rendered by Rhys Davids and myself as craving (or sometimes, poetically, by "thirst"). It stands always for natural, unregenerate desire and impulse. In pursuing the final ideal, all *kāma's* (both forms and objects of this natural craving), whether they be earthly or heavenly, are reckoned as hindrances.

But strenuous volition was too vitally essential in the Buddhist scheme of regeneration to be made coincident only with *tanhā*. To the pilgrim in the Four Paths, all *kāma* had become transformed into aspirations and purposes called *sammā-sankappa* (supreme or right design or aspiration), and *dhamma-chanda* (normal desire or intention). *Chanda* is paraphrased by "state-of-desire to do." It is sometimes made to take the place of *tanhā*. For instance, *dukkha* is said to be "rooted in *chanda*,"[2] as indeed, elsewhere, all states of consciousness are said to be.[3] And in one passage the Buddha's system of holy living is called the removal of *chanda*.

[1] With Rhys Davids I do not call these, as most translators do, "hells" (*niraya*), because there was no eternal life in them any more than in the heavens.

[2] *Samyutta-N.*, iv. 328.

[3] *Anguttara-N.*, iv. 339.

But note the context. This very removal is to be accomplished through the agency of *chanda*. The inquiring Brahmin asks the Elder, Ānanda, how *chanda* is to be got rid of. Ānanda repeats the discipline, included in the "wisdom-winged states," in which will (*chanda*), energy and investigation are to be developed. "But how," is the comment, "will you put away *chanda* by *chanda*?" The Elder replies: "Was there not desire, effort, intelligence and deliberation in your mind, when you set out to question me in this park? And now that you have found me, is not all that abated?"[1]

Many other passages might be quoted to show that eager, determined *chanda* is the essential and chief criterion of a genuine *sekha*, or candidate for Arahantship. Hence (as I have said elsewhere [2]) "it is strictly in accordance with the spirit of the older writings, if with an added tinge of intense emotion, when the author of the *Milinda* declares that Nibbāna is to be realized, not by quiescent meditation only, nor in hypnotic trance, much less by mortification of desire, but by rational discontent, strong anguish, longing, followed by a forward leap of the mind into peace and calm, then again by a vibrating zeal, in which the aspirant strives with might and main along the path," etc. [3]

[1] *Samyutta-N.*, v. 272.
[2] *Dictionary of Religion and Ethics*, "Desire."
[3] ii. 199 f.

That Buddhism should be so often described as teaching "extinction of desire," without due qualification in such a statement, results not only from want of knowledge concerning the scope and grades of a doctrine, which was for all sorts and conditions of men, but also from the fact that the two pioneer translators of Buddhist anthologies were neither English nor psychologically trained.[1] Between them they have rendered no fewer than sixteen Pāli words of varying import by the one word desire, the sixteen all referring to forms of vicious or excessive desire. And the views of philosophical and popularizing writers have suffered distortion accordingly.

In the third grade of the higher training, we note, taking both definitions, that the object and end of the training is such mental emancipation, or liberty as enables the subject to know things as they really or truly are.

The last expression is of considerable interest, as I have elsewhere endeavoured to show.[2] It is no hole and corner phrase, but runs right through three of the four chief Nikāyas. It reminds us at once of Matthew Arnold's definition of the mission and ideal of literary criticism: the "endeavour to see the object as in itself it really is," or "things

[1] Max Müller and Fausböll, S.B.E. x.; so St. Hilaire, Burnouf, Foucaux, with *désir*.

[2] *Psychological Ethics*, lxviii.; *Buddhism* (Rangoon), 1904, "Seeing things as they really are."

as they really are." Much, for that matter, in Arnold's thoughts is soundly Buddhist, and in pathetic contrast to his ignorance of Buddhism. His famous line, so pertinent to this very ideal:

> Who saw life steadily and saw it whole,

reads almost as an echo of a Buddhist verse on the Master:—

> He hath discernèd all this life o' the world,
> In all the world the how and thus of things,
> From all detached and leaning upon naught;
> Who all hath mastered, from all bonds is loosed:
> Touched is for him high peace and the blest calm,[1]
> Where no fear cometh more.

It is impossible to render the phrase *yathā-bhūta*m literally, for so it means "according-as-become." A kindred expression in Greek for fact or truth is *ge-*, *gig-no mena*, the "come-to-be" or "happened"; anyway the meaning of the Pāli is clear enough and the phrase is peculiarly Buddhist. It does not occur in any Upanishad, nor in such of the ancient Jain documents as have been edited, although pasages are not infrequent where a Buddhist compiler would have inserted it. If we consult the Nikāyas to see what are the things that should be seen and known as they really are, we find, in one Nikāya alone, the following range of subjects. Not only the nature, cause, and abolition of ill or suffering, but also—

[1] Nibbāna. *Anguttara-Nikāya*, ii. 24.

The nature and impermanence of the external world and everything in it;

The nature and impermanence of personality or the individual compound;

The non-existence of a permanent, transmigrating soul;

The universality of cause and effect;

The nature of good, one's own and others';

The nature of moral and intellectual emancipation, *etc.*

I do not think it accurate to force the significance of the Buddhists' using "become" where Arnold in this our day said "are." Yet when we find *bhūta*m used in place of the usual "arising" or "cause": *samūd'ăya*, we have some excuse in ascribing significance to the accompanying *yathā-bhūta*m. "This has come to be (*bhūta*m), Sāriputta, do you see? This has become, Sāriputta, do you see?" "It has become, master; by right insight one sees it *even as it has become* (*yathābhūta*n)."[1]

The capacity for regarding things, even the apparently most statical and permanent, even soul and deity, under this aspect, was made by the Buddha the criterion of a right grasp of his philosophy. Such an one is

[1] *Samyutta-Nikāya*, ii. 48; cf. *Majjhima-Nikāya*, i. 260. That we have lost our strong Saxon *weorthan*, and have to make shift with the weak 'become,' blurred by other implications, puts us at a disadvantage in Pāli as compared with Germans, who have retained their *werden*, and with the French, whose *devenir* M. Bergson is wielding with such Buddhist emphasis.

called *sankhāta-dhamma,* "one who has reckoned up things,"[1] and *a-sekha,* adept, non-learner (*i.e.,* Arahant). And the standpoint includes four points: (1) *x* has come to be (as effect of a cause). (2) Because of specific conditions, or nutriment. (3) *x* ceases with the exhaustion of that nutriment. (4) He who thus sees ceases to be subject, or devoted, to *x*. In other words, he gains another step in emancipation, or independence of heart and mind.

Now we have seen that saintly Buddhists, who realized their ideal, conceived it in a variety of ways. But here, I contend, is truth put forward as an ideal in a way unsurpassed for earnestness by any other ancient movement of thought. It is possible that Dr. Wundt[2] pronounced truth to be the Buddhist ideal from the fact that the fundamental doctrine of Ill and its cessation, together with the "Eightfold Path" thereto, is formulated as the Four Ariyan Truths. This necessity of seeing things as they truly have become is therefore additional evidence supporting his view, a view which I would only modify by ranking Truth as one, and not the sole, ideal of Buddhism.

Truth is immortal speech, the everlasting Norm.
On NORM and GOOD and TRUTH the saint hath ta'en his
stand.[3]

---

[1] *Sutta-Nipāta,* 1038.

[2] *Völker psychologie,* ii. 3, 720.

[3] *Samyutta-Nikāya,* i. 189.

The Pāli word which I have rendered "insight" is but one of the many terms for mental activity and attainment built, in Indian tongues, on the roots "to know" and "to see." Our European languages are not rich enough in terms of higher intelligence to produce equivalents. Perhaps our religious ideals have tended to be emotional rather than intellectual. For instance, *ñāna* may mean any knowledge, from trivial to highest. But *aññā* means only the highest, while *paññā* and *abhiññā* express the active intelligence expanding in that direction. Equally numerous are the terms for clarity of mental vision.

Finally, with respect to the nature of the "emancipation" essential to Arahantship, *vimutti* is not only a Buddhist ideal, but one advocated by Indian philosophical creeds very generally. But it was conceived, as subjective experience, variously. In animistic creeds, it was held to be the result of realizing the detachment of soul from all connection with matter. And it was experienced in one creed as bliss, in another as total unconsciousness, and so on.[1] Buddhism conceived various channels debouching in emancipation. There was that mentioned above as the destruction of the intoxicants[2] (*khīnāsava*, "one who has the *āsava's* destroyed," is a common synonym for Arahant). Or it is "craving,"

[1] R. Garbe, *Die Sānkhya-Philosophie*, pp. 323-25.
[2] *Samyutta-Nik.*, v. 410.

that is destroyed.[1] Or it is by examining and turning away from all theories and aspirations as to possible celestial realms of rebirth. This is termed emancipation by insight.[2]

> And see, O Master! Sundarī who comes
> To tell thee of Emancipation won,
> And of the right no more to be reborn;
> Who hath herself from passion freed,
> Unyoked from bondage, loosened from the world.[3]

Or there is the emancipation of the heart or mind through love: "All the means that can be used as bases for doing right are not worth one sixteenth part of the emancipation of the heart through love. That takes all those up into itself, outshining them in radiance and in glory."[4] Similarly there was emancipation of heart through the other three sublime moods named above.

In later Abhidhamma, the realization of the three salient features, signs or marks, characterizing all phenomena, was pictured as a threefold avenue to emancipation. These were the absence of soul, the presence of Ill, and the absence of permanence. To make this doctrine impressive, striking adjectives were selected to characterize the emancipated state; things as soulless were "empty"—void of soul—to realize this was "Empty-Release." Things as transient had no sign or mark of permanence—to realize this was

[1] *Anguttara-N.* ii. 1.
[2] *Dialogues*, ii. 68.
[3] *Psalms of the Sisters*, 140.
[4] *Iti-vuttaka*, 19.

"No-lasting-sign-Release." Things as involving suffering were not to be hankered after—to realize this was "End-of-baneful-longing-Release." These are uncouth names to us, and a plucking at lax strings that give out no resonance. But even a Bunyan would need the sounding-board of a Buddhist tradition to devise names that could stir our hearts, as these have doubtless vibrated in the Buddhist religious consciousness.

And it is no dirge that these three chords give out, strange as this may seem to many among us. It was not the Buddhist laity alone who could live happily and look forward with confidence. He too, or she, who had wearied of both the bravery and the squalor of life, even of the horizons of a happy sequel, who had sickened with the divine distemper heralding the final victory, who had staked all and won—

> In whom the Asavas are dried up . . .
> Whose range is in the Void and th' Unmarked,
> And Liberty. . . .[1]

for these their goal and their memories are girt about with deep wells of joy. "Dwelling in the rapture, the bliss, the joy, of emancipation, of fruition, of Nibbāna"—when pondering the distinction, the attainment to which they had come:—in such phrases run the various records.

"It is in very bliss we dwell," runs a psalm of the Norm, "we who hate not those who

[1] *Psalms of the Brethren*, xcii.

hate us . . . we in health among the ailing . . . free from care among the careworn . . . we who have no hindrances; we shall become feeders on rapture" (*pīti-bhakkhā*[1]) . . . (*Compendium*, 243.) Mr. Aung earnestly dissents, as a scrupulously accurate translator, from the usual rendering of *pīti* by joy, or any purely *emotional* term. The word, he writes, means *interest*, in which Buddhists distinguish five degrees of intensity, up to thrill and rapture. It is the intellectual excitement in an object felt as desirable. If, however, with M. Bergson, we assign to "joy," as distinct from "pleasure," the lofty meaning of intellectual rapture and triumph over intuitive and creative work,[2] then is "joy" not far wrong for the *pīti* of high intensity that inspires these Arahant efforts to express their sense of vision and of victory, as one after another, "experiencing the bliss of emancipation," he or she utters or "breathes out" some verse:—

> Now have they prospered, all my highest aims,
> To compass which I sought this still retreat.
> The holy lore and Liberty, my quest,
> Shone clear when vain conceits were cast away.
>
> * * * *
>
> I what 'twas well to do have done, and what
> Is verily delectable, therein
> Was my delight; and thus through happiness
> Has happiness been sought after and won.[3]

---

[1] *Dhammapada*, ver. 197-200.

[2] *Hibbert Journal*, Oct., 1911: "Life and Consciousness."

[3] *Psalms of the Brethren*, lx., lxiii.

To some then even the quest and its disciplines were happiness; to others, in the words of Nāgasena,[1] whereas Nibbāna is all bliss unalloyed, the process of seeking after it involves pain. But the state itself is realized in consciousness "by freedom from distress and danger, by confidence, by peace, by calm, by bliss, by happiness, by sweetness, by purity, by coolness."[2]

How strange is the intellectual landscape —to repeat Henry Warren's phrase—coloured by these emotions, when compared with that of other religious anthologies! Nibbāna is likened, with glowing eloquence, by Nāgasena to a wonderful city of the Norm—*dhamma-năgără*—built for mankind by the Buddha as architect, lit up by the Norm, with moral conduct for its ramparts, prudence for its moat, knowledge for its gate-battlements, energy for its watch-tower, and bazaars where men come to exchange their karma for the intellectual and spiritual requisites of the Arahant.

But this "glorious city, stainless and undefiled, pure and white, ageless, deathless, secure, calm and happy" is no place in earth or heaven. "There is no spot, O king, East, South, West or North, above, below or beyond, where Nibbāna is situate, and yet Nibbāna is, and he who orders his life aright, grounded in virtue, and with rational attention, may realize it, whether he live in Greece, China

[1] *Milinda*, ii. 182 f. [2] *Ibid.*, 196.

Alexandria or in Kôsălă." For he enters that city who "emancipates his mind in Arahantship."[1]

Even were it clear, from the saintly rhapsodies of Buddhist scriptures, that this present Nibbāna was the threshold of an ageless, spaceless and generally inconceivable yet positive state of being, it is not a little wonderful that the early saints, many of them persons of no more culture and learning than were the majority of the early Christians, should have so loyally refrained from speculating about, and exulting over, it as a positive event *in the future.*

There is, in fact, in this literature of Buddhist saintship, a very wholesome corrective to narrowness of view respecting what may or may not suffice for the goal of religious aspiration. It is impossible to know the literature and yet be sceptical as to the faith, the enthusiasm and the emotion being as ardent as may be found in any religious literature. We may well wonder over it; but we may no less "thank whatever gods there be" for this phase of the unconquerable spirit of man, who, while realizing the unutterable vastness in length and breadth of life, could not only claim to cut himself free from it, but could also see, in the process, a moral and intellectual apotheosis to that life, and could hail it with a very swan's song of saintly rapture.

[1] *Milinda*, 212 f.; 202 f.

CHAPTER IX

THE IMPORT OF DHAMMA

LET it be clearly understood that, in evolving an outline of the fundamental postulates of Buddhism from the Commentator's exposition of the term Dhamma, I have not gone the orthodox way to work. This way would doubtless have been, with my esteemed collaborator, Mr. S. Z. Aung, to state the gist of Buddhist philosophy in the three propositions:—"All things are impermanent . . . pain-engendering . . . without soul." *Kamma-niyama*, he would add, is included in the doctrine of becoming-by-way-of cause; and this again is included in the first two propositions. (I quote from a letter.)

But I write, in the first place, for Western readers, to whom these corner-stones of Buddhist tradition and the lie of them are unfamiliar. And I trust that, like those swift messengers from the West in the story,[1] this heterodox method of presentation may reach the crossways of consciousness and be admitted as bearing a no less trustworthy tale. As a recast, it may not be without suggestiveness.

[1] Page 180f.

The meaning of Dhamma most familiar to us :—that of Teaching, Word, Doctrine—is as expressive and as weighty as are the corresponding words, or The Gospel, to a Christian, the Law to a Jew. For all Buddhists of whatever branch Dhamma or Dharma stands, with those other two, Buddha and Sangha (Order, Church or Fraternity), as the unique gem-trinity—Răt'ănăttăyă—or supreme categories of Buddhist devotion and reverence. And as there have been, in this world and its forerunners in the eternal universe, previous Buddhas each with his Sangha, so have there been previous Pitakas containing the eternally renewed teaching of the Norm. The chronicles of Dhammapāla, *e.g.*, of the fifth (?) century, A.D., relate of Pu*nn*ā, one of the first women-apostles, that in a previous birth, when Vipassi was Buddha, she "had learnt the Three Pitakas and taught the Norm." [1]

The meaning of the word *dhamma*, as norm, standard or rule, is perhaps best shown in the interesting Aggañña or Genesis Discourse.[2] I give an outline of it here on that account. It is a striking specimen of archaic science attempting a rational theory of the origin of human institutions.

The Buddha has been asking two young Brahmins, who have left all to follow him, how their class has judged of their decision. They tell him the Brahmins are scandalized at their

[1] *Psalms of the Sisters,* 116.

[2] *Dialogues,* iii., No. xxvii. ; *cf.* i. 105-7.

leaving their class:—the true aristocrats, clear-complexioned, pure descendants and heirs of the great god Brahmā—to follow shaveling friar-folk of a lower class. The Buddha then proceeds to show, first that such talk is very "high-faluting," inasmuch as Brahmin children are obviously of very human birth, and that no social class or caste (literally, colour) had a monopoly of pure or impure living. A man was only pronounced perfect or holy, who, no matter what his class, had satisfied a certain norm of holy attainment. For it is ever a norm that determines what is best.

"For instance the king of Kosala shows me reverence only because I have attained to a certain standard, to which he knows he has not attained. In honouring me, he honours a norm. So you two, when men ask, 'Who are you?' say ye, 'We are recluses of the Sākyans, sons of the Exalted One, born from his mouth, born of the Norm, created by the Norm, heirs of the Norm.' And why? Because such names as these: belonging to the Norm, or to the Highest; and again, One with the Norm, or the Highest, are tantamount to Tathāgata."[1]

He then goes on after this sort:—"There comes a time when this earth passes away, beings having been reborn elsewhere. There

[1] The name applied to his office and mission by the Buddha, and meaning "The Thus-come" or "Thus-gone." See also p. 193.

comes also a time when this world begins to evolve once more, all having become water and dark, a darkness to make you blind. And beings deceasing from radiant worlds are reborn, self-luminous on this earth, sustained by rapture, floating in space. As earth emerges from the waters like a milky scum or ghee, odorous and sweet, those beings taste it. Feasting thereon, they gradually acquire solidity and lose their own luminance. Thereupon sun, moon and stars become visible, and the natural seasons recommence. And this race of beings acquire different degrees of comeliness; and the fair despise the ugly. And thereupon the earth ceases to taste sweet, but vegetation of low, then higher grade evolves, till at length the earth brings forth abundance of a rice that needs no tilth. Then sex-differences evolve, and great moral upheavals result. As households come into being, rice is stored, land is enclosed, and with the rights of property arise dishonesty, strife and injustice, till at length a ruler is chosen to maintain fair play, the rest supporting him. And he is selected for his personal gifts; in other words such lords of the *fields* (*khetta, khattiya*), came up originally to a certain Norm. Or again, as princes, they *attracted* folk (*rāja*; *rañj*) by the Norm they upheld. Again, certain humans, distressed at the sins of society, retire into woods to meditate, or dwell outside the towns, making books (*sic*). Now these, putting away (*bāhenti*) evil, came to be called *Brah-*

mins. Them also men distinguished from others, solely because, in thought, word, deed they came up to a certain human Norm. Others again, leading domestic lives and proficient (*vissutā*) in certain industries, thereby fulfilling a different standard, are called Vessas, and others again, passed muster only in minor or low crafts (*khudda*), and became known as Suddas, these too only differing from other people by a certain Norm.

"Now there comes a time when a Khattiya, a Brahmin, Vessa, or Sudda, misprizing his own Norm, goes forth from his home into the homeless life, saying: 'I will become a recluse.' And thus the class of recluses comes into being, differing from others only in the possession of a special Norm. If these are good they are reborn in a happy heavenly world; if bad, into misery; if both good and bad, into a future of mixed happiness and misery. If a Khattiya, or one of the other three groups, is self-restrained in deed, word and thought, has followed the practice of the seven priciples which are the Wings of Wisdom (*bodhipakkhiyā dhammā*), he attains to complete extinction of evil in this present life. And of these four groups, the one who, as a bhikkhu, is Arahant, who has destroyed all moral taint, who has wrought his whole duty, who has laid down the burden, who has won his own salvation, who has wholly broken off the fetter of rebirth (literally: of becoming), who through knowledge made perfect is free—

he is declared to be chief in virtue of a Norm.

"For a Norm is what men call highest, both for this life and the next."

"We may not," comments Rhys Davids[1] on the legend of this Dialogue, "accept its historical accuracy. Indeed a continual note of good-humoured irony runs through the whole story, with its fanciful etymologies of the names of the four classes, or 'colours' (*vannā*); and the aroma of it would be lost on the hearer who took it quite seriously. But it reveals a sound and healthy insight, and is much nearer to the actual facts than the Brahmin legend it was intended to replace." For our immediate purpose its chief interest lies in its explication of the import of Dhamma, as primarily norm, or standard. Khattiyas might be distinguished as originally administrators of justice; Brahmins, as originally followers of religious, pure, or righteous lives. But the *dhamma* of the other two classes was indisputably their proficiency in certain secular unmoral arts and crafts. Hence, whereas Dhamma may imply righteousness, justice, truth, virtue, law, its most fundamental meaning is more general, being "that on account of which"—be it righteousness, or some *un*moral proficiency—a distinction is assigned, in other words a rule, test, standard or norm.

[1] *Dialogues*, i. 107.

CONCLUSION

In this slight and very inadequate study of the Buddhist Dhamma, interpreted as a doctrine of the Norm, I have connected it, by way of the allied terms *dhammatā*, normness, and *niyāmatā*, governance, with the Buddhist concept of a fivefold *niyama* or order, observable in the universe. Whether we contemplate Buddhism as a religion, or as a normative or practical philosophy (ethics), or whether we inquire into the fundamental inductions implicated in its practical doctrine, we can see everywhere the notion of a cosmos,—external world and internal experience—proceeding as incessant flux, without beginning, without ending, inexorable, necessary. We have seen that in this cosmos, or cosmic order, room is found for a *kamma-niyama*, or law of what we should call moral action, namely, that thoughts, words and deeds of sentient beings which are of a nature to produce results on sentience will produce such results, either on the agent in this life, or by re-creating him, or otherwise affecting him in other lives.

Into the *niyama* of material processes, as elaborated by mediæval Buddhism, our knowledge of the scholastic literature is yet too immature to warrant our entering here. It may be gathered in outline from the little manual *Compendium of Philosophy*.[1] Allusion will also be found in that work to theories of space and of time, and to the threefold rhythm, in time as in life itself, of a nascent, a static and a cessant phase.

We saw, finally, that in the universal order, a *dhamma-niyama* was distinguished, that is to say, the law of nature concerned with the evolution of a perfect type or super-man. Buddhists would probably admit that this included all Arahants, as differing from a Buddha only in degree of powers and attainments. But the law is cited (see above, page [120) only in reference to a Buddha. It implies a serial, organic tendency in the universe towards a normal or perfect type. By the thought and action of this culminating type of individual the upward tendency in the many is held to be greatly forwarded, the rise being considerable during his lifetime, subsequently less. By upward tendency is here meant, it need hardly be said, better conformity, in character and conduct, to the moral law or kamma-order. The acts of mankind become more prevailingly such as have *pleasant* results.

This betterment lasts for some centuries. Gotama Buddha allowed ten centuries for his *sad-dhamma*, good law, gospel, or Norm as

[1] Pp. 154, 250, 271.

revealed by him, to stand, but five centuries only, when he conceded that women should be admitted as members of his Fraternity. And so far as Indian Buddhism is concerned, the prophecy was fulfilled in a period about midway between the two dates. By that time, at least, the *sad-dhamma* was no longer standing firm. That his great thought and work of love had, by that time, perished and left no impress on countless numbers of his fellows is not meant here, and doubtless was not meant originally. Here however we are concerned with the width and sweep of the Buddhist conception of law, or world-order. Not even so immense and culminating an event as that of the world's redemption and salvation was by it considered as unique. No fiat uttered once for all :—" I will send my only-begotten Son "—was admissible in a cosmodicy that was eternal. Everything could happen ; nothing could be unique. And so the Niyama-scheme included even this :—the strand, the golden thread of a Dhamma-order, an order which the other four strands of nature toiled for ages to foster and minister to, an order which was the articulate expression of the five-fold order itself—the human life of perfect knowledge and service lived by a Saviour-Buddha. There were held to be frequent approximations to this perfect type : men who attained to great knowledge, through vision of many things past finding out by ordinary mortals. But they were wise each man for himself alone, and so were called Pacche'ka-Buddhas. They lacked the power or the temperament to teach. And this was reckoned as a relative lack of knowledge, since the Buddha who devotes his life to helping mankind was termed, not Saviour, but Omniscient (*sabbaññu*) Buddha. To understand all, says a French epigram, is to forgive all. The Buddhist goes farther; to understand all, is not only to forgive, but to give—to give one's self through insight into others' need. Pacche'ka-Buddhas and even Arahants may in these days be hard to find. But that a Buddha named Metteyya should in the fulness of time arise, is recorded in the Canon as a prophecy made by Gotama himself.

We, in this Buddhantără, or interim age, may witness no such auspicious advent. But some of us may yet live to see a niche assigned to Buddhism as a philosophic tradition among other such traditions, ancient and mediæval, either credited with originality, or at least admitted, on evidence considerably more sound than any that has yet been brought forward, as an interesting evolution of some genuinely prior group of thinkers. In its mother-land, Buddhism, in mediæval and modern times, has stood as little chance of being appreciated by Indian philosophers, as experimental, evolutionary or pluralistic philosophy is likely to be approved of by students nourished on Thomas Aquinas. And those thinkers who with trend of thought more in sympathy with that of Buddhism, have been and are casting our traditional standpoints into the crucible to re-construct them, have as yet thought and taught without access to their Buddhist prototypes of an earlier age. In so far, however, as these thinkers—I may instance James, Bergson and Alexander—represent a flowing tide in the affairs of philosophy, their work and influence will aid, whether they know it or not, in securing a just and more sympathetic appraisement for Buddhist Abhidhamma, when the literature has been more fully presented and adequately discussed by scholars from the West and also from the East.

Till this comes to pass, fuller recognition cannot be expected, or even desired, so many and so pathetic are the mistaken conclusions due to scanty knowledge and the attitude of a different tradition. As an instance let this suffice. In the *Indian Antiquary*, not long ago, a writer, trained in Catholic scholastic philosophy, took writers on Buddhism to task for making the Buddha, " who had a thorough knowledge of the metaphysic of his time," proclaim, in the theory of the groups (*khandha's*) a tissue of absurdities. For the Buddha knew well enough that " accidents must be inherent in a substance in order to possess any reality at all. He could not have taken quality for essence without making himself the laughing-stock of those around him. To teach an incongruous jumble of subjectless attributes is a unthinkable as a suit of clothes walking about without a wearer."

We can imagine a Buddhist well amused at this fancy of *ātman* shivering or shamed and most needy. But the point for us is, that the Buddha, for all the knowledge here allowed him, did and does seem to teach a tissue of absurdities to those of every age and tradition, who can only conceive things and beings as "substances having qualities." The Bauddhas, as the Indian Absolutists called them, disallowed that this was the true way of conception, and averred that it was the standpoint of the unlearned *puthuj'jănă*, or "many-folk." To their opponents, on the other hand, Becoming seemed irrational beside Being. "How can that which is proceed from that which is not?" Or "how can you build upon nothing?" the Vedântist will say, as if building on a basis were now the most fundamental aspect of reality. It is so only in an idiom which sprang from a belief now superseded. The argument is founded on the Ptolemaic conception of the earth's fixity in space, with all the heavens revolving about it. Yet while we held both Ptolemaic view and idiom, while in India at the back of men's speech lurked the old myth of the world resting on elephant or tortoise, this same earth, seeming so fundamentally stable, was engaged in an encyclical choric dance, with never anything in her of an ultimate fundamental basis. Copernicus taught us that, in the very nature of things, there can be no fundamental basis, no permanent fixity. Was this perhaps what Buddhism was feeling after, when it caught hold of a three-fold rhythm in life and time, and pictured causation not as a mechanical succession of moments, but as one moment or state being wrought up into, and informing the next with a ceaseless pulsation ?

Anti-Ptolemaic it was further in this respect that it was not, in its Theravādin tradition, ego-centric. It is the weakness of Idealistic systems, Professor Alexander has reminded us,[1] to consist in endeavours, not to interpret disinterestedly, and independently of self, but to see in or experience, ultimately, constructions of mind or self. The Buddhistic attitude, on the contrary, loses the temporary self in the object, so that the cosmos, without and within, is ultimately Object, the subject (or self) being termed in this connection, "objectic" (*ārammanika*).[2] The object is the relater, the subject is the related.

"Let us faithfully and patiently cultivate the dawning 'Copernican' consciousness": —namely, that ultimate reality and "our supreme and vital need" is no fixed basis nor moveless central stand, but throbbing energies whirling in ordered rhythm, whether of solar

[1] *Hibbert Journal,* Oct. 1909: "Ptolemaic and Copernican views of the place of mind in the universe."

[2] S. Z. Aung, *op. cit.*, p. 2

systems or our own hearts and intelligences, the consciousness of a dynamical order replacing that of a statical order; a Way of life, which, like the spinning globe, bears no forward on its bosom, more swiftly than we can journey on it; so that "beyond our best there ever rises a better hope."[1] Such seems to me the end and outcome of Buddhist philosophy, even if neither its earlier nor its later teachers formulated it in terms for which we have to thank the great re-creation of our science achieved in the seventeenth century. If it be objected that the philosophic ideal of Buddhism is calm and peace, the obvious answer is that calm and peace are the attributes of harmonious rhythm—of one who like the Most High "rides upon the storm," of one whose mind is not overwhelmed or harassed by its discernment of change, movement, becoming, as the truly real, but which masters its vision. In an age of evolutionary science and of increasing and habitual swift physical movement, such notions are brought near to us. It was a great and pioneer fetch of the mind to have disposed thought towards dynamical concepts under the conditions obtaining over 2,000 years ago.

And when we watch the way in which Gotama Buddha and his followers met the errors and the problems of their own day, recasting,

[1] Lady Welby; quoted in Sir E. Arnold's *Death—and Afterwards* (1887). The anonymity I have her kind, if reluctantly given permission to remove.

it may be, a yet more ancient body of doctrine to cope with present needs, can we doubt that, if a Metteyya Buddha arose here and now, he would recast their Dhamma, and, instead of making "converts" to a Norm adapted to bygone conditions, would evolve, with travail of soul, a gospel and a philosophy built out of the knowledge and the needs of to-day? In these slight studies the effort has been made to follow R. L. Stevenson's advice[1] and present the subject-matter from within, with something of the actor's sympathy. But the conviction is also present that, for convinced Buddhists of to-day, who stand on the threshold of a great crisis, as well as for scholars in general, an inquiry into the bases of ancient Buddhist thought may become a living force in present evolution, even as the explorer, carving a way to the forward view, turns to adjust his bearings by some rearward range of hills with kindred trend.

[1] See above, p. 109.

CHRONOLOGICAL NOTE

SIXTH CENTURY B.C. Probable period of Go'tama Buddha's life and work. The orthodox Ceylon tradition (recorded in the metrical chronicles *Mahāvamsa* and *Dīpavamsa*—the "great" and the "island" chronicle—place the birth of Go'tama late in the 7th century B.C., *viz.*, in 624, and his death (Parinibbāna) in B.C. 544. Thus the year 1912 is, for Buddhists, 2456 B.E. (Buddhist Era). These dates are obtained by reckoning backwards the sum of the years assigned to each Ceylon king's reign, recorded in the chronicles, till Asoka's son Mahinda introduced Buddhism into Ceylon. This is dated in the eighteenth year after Asoka's coronation, and in the first year of the reign of Devānam-piya-Tissa (Tissa, beloved of gods) King of Ceylon. Asoka is further stated to have been crowned "two hundred and eighteen years after the Parinibbāna of the Sambuddha."

Now this method of reckoning fractions of years, when reigns began or ended, as whole years, obviously stretches the interval, after a time, to an appreciable extent. It is unfortunately impossible to say exactly to what extent. But historical critics have a rough corrective in the important rock-cut edicts of Asoka. In one of these, insoribed both at Kapur di Giri on the Indus in Kashmir, and at Khauli on the Jumna, near Masuri, Asoka refers to neighbouring rulers :—Antiyoka (Antiochus) Yona raja (King of Greece), "and beyond him four kings, Tulamaye (Ptolemy), Antikina (Antiochus), Mākā (Magas), and Alikasandare (Alexander)." Working by this and other clues, it is judged that a more accurate *approximate* date for the eighty to eighty-one years of the Buddha's life is 563-483 B.C.

NOTE to p. 32. The criticism to which this theory exposes itself through lack of sound historical evidence, and through lack of adequate internal testimony to its alleged dependence, has been administered in outline by Rhys Davids (*American Lectures on Buddhism*, 1896, 24-6), and more fully by H. Oldenberg (*Buddha*, 5th ed., 65-71, which summarizes prior, more detailed discussion. See *fn.*).

BIBLIOGRAPHY

CANONICAL AUTHORITIES

OF the Pali Pitakas the Vinaya Pitaka is nearly all translated (Rhys Davids and Oldenberg), in *Sacred Books of the East*, xiii., xvii., xx. as *Vinaya Texts.* The Sutta Pitaka contains, in the four Nikāyas or collections:—*Dīgha*, *Majjhima*, *Samyutta*, *Anguttara*—practically the whole body of early doctrine. The first two are in process of being translated by Rhys Davids and myself, as *Dialogues of the Buddha.* The last two are as yet untranslated. Dr. Neumann has translated the Majjhima into German. Bhikkhu Nyānatiloka has translated a portion of the Anguttara into German. Other translated portions of the Pitaka are *Buddhist Suttas*, S.B.E. xi. by Rhys Davids; Dhammapada and Sutta-Nipāta, S.B.E. x., Max Müller and Fausböll. *Iti-Vuttaka*, as *Sayings of Buddha*, by J. Moore, 1908. *Udāna*, by D. M. Strong, 1902. *Psalms of the Early Buddhists*, by the writer, 1909, 1912. *The Jātaka*, by R. Chalmers, W. Rouse, etc., 1895-1907.

Of the Abhidhamma-Pitaka only the first book has been translated, as *Buddhist Psychological Ethics*, by the writer, 1900. Bhikkhu Nyānatiloka has translated another book, the *Puggala-Paññatti*, into German, as *Das Buch der Charaktere*, 1910.

LATER PALI WORKS

The Questions of King Milinda, translated by Rhys Davids, S.B.E. xxxv, xxxvi.

The *Mahāvamsa,* translated by Professor W. Geiger and Mrs. Bode, 1912.

The *Dīpavamsa,* translated by Professor H. Oldenberg, 1879.

Compendium of Philosophy, a mediæval digest of Abhidhamma, translated by S. Z. Aung and the writer, 1910.

(No other mediæval works have as yet been translated.)

Of works on India in Buddhist times the reader may consult :—

Buddhist India, by Rhys Davids (The Stories of the Nations), 2nd ed. 1904.

The Early History of India, by Vincent Smith, 2nd. ed., 1909.

History of India, for senior classes, Part I., by E. Marsden, 1909.

On Yuan Chwang, by T. Watters, 1904-5.

Phonetic note.—The upright "m" in italicized Pāli names, or *vice versa, e.g., Samyutta,* is pronounced "ng." The upright (or italicized) n does not affect pronunciation appreciably. To aid pronunciation, and to harass the reader as little as possible with unfamiliar marks, the transliteration, in other respects, is not meticulously accurate. *Chitta,* e.g., should be *citta.*

INDEX